EZEKIEL AMONG THE PROPHETS

STUDIES IN BIBLICAL THEOLOGY

A series of monographs designed to provide the best work in biblical scholarship both in this country and abroad

Advisory Editors:

STUDIES IN BIBLICAL THEOLOGY

Second Series · 31

EZEKIEL AMONG THE PROPHETS

A Study of Ezekiel's Place in Prophetic Tradition

KEITH W. CARLEY

ALEC R. ALLENSON INC.
635 EAST OGDEN AVENUE
NAPERVILLE, ILL.

© *SCM Press Ltd*

ISBN 0-8401-3081-3

Library of Congress Catalog Card No. 74-23023

224.4
C 19e
93238
april 1975

Published by Alec R. Allenson Inc.
Naperville, Ill.
Printed in Great Britain

CONTENTS

PREFACE

If only by reason of its length, the book of Ezekiel is an important part of the Old Testament. There has been a great deal of writing about Ezekiel in scholarly and also in popular works this century. But for many readers of the Old Testament Ezekiel remains a puzzling book. This study attempts to solve some of the problems by examining influences that bore upon Ezekiel as he undertook his prophetic calling. It is based upon a London University Ph.D thesis completed in 1968. Other commitments have prevented earlier preparation of the material for publication. In Papua New Guinea there is not the range of current literature available for as thorough a revision as I would have wished. On the other hand the many arresting parallels between Israelite and Melanesian culture have given a broader basis for understanding Ezekiel's thought-world, and I trust the study still represents a relevant contribution to the contemporary reassessment of the prophet.

The thesis was written under the supervision of the Rev Professor P. R. Ackroyd of King's College, London. His advice and encouragement have also led to the preparation of the present work for publication, though this does not necessarily imply he is in agreement with the views expressed in it. As the notes will indicate I am also indebted to numerous other scholars, whether their works are referred to critically or in support of some aspect of an argument. But Professor W. Zimmerli's studies on Ezekiel, from which the thesis originated, have been particularly helpful. My gratitude is also due to Dr M. A. Knibb of King's College, London, for advice regarding the pseudepigraphic material referred to in chapter II; to the editor and advisers of the SCM Press for advice in preparing this volume; and to my wife for her considerable assistance in typing and indexing the manuscript.

Rarongo Theological College   K. W. CARLEY
Papua New Guinea
May 1974

ABBREVIATIONS

AB	Anchor Bible, New York
AJSL	*American Journal of Semitic Languages and Literatures,* Chicago, Ill.
ANVAO	Avhandlinger utgitt av Det Norske Videnskaps-Akademi i Oslo, II, Hist.-Filos. Klasse, Oslo
ASTI	*Annual of the Swedish Theological Institute in Jerusalem,* Leiden
ATD	Das Alte Testament Deutsch, Göttingen
AThANT	Abhandlungen zur Theologie des Alten und Neuen Testaments, Zürich
BA	*The Biblical Archaeologist* (New Haven, Conn.), Cambridge, Mass.
BDB	F. Brown, S. R. Driver and C. A. Briggs, *A Hebrew and English Lexicon of the Old Testament,* Oxford 1907
BHTh	Beiträge zur Historischen Theologie, Tübingen
BJRL	*Bulletin of the John Rylands Library,* Manchester
BKAT	Biblischer Kommentar: Altes Testament, Neukirchen
BL	H. Bauer and P. Leander, *Historische Grammatik der hebräischen Sprache des Alten Testaments,* Halle 1922
BWANT	Beiträge zur Wissenschaft vom Alten und Neuen Testament (Leipzig), Stuttgart
BZAW	Beihefte zur *Zeitschrift für die Alttestamentliche Wissenschaft* (Giessen), Berlin
EH	Exegetisches Handbuch zum Alten Testament, Münster
ET	English translation
EvTh	*Evangelische Theologie,* München
FRLANT	Forschungen zur Religion und Literatur des Alten und Neuen Testaments, Göttingen
GK	W. Gesenius, E. Kautzsch, *Hebrew Grammar,* ET Oxford ²1910
HAT	Handbuch zum Alten Testament, Tübingen
HK	Handkommentar zum Alten Testament, Göttingen
HUCA	*Hebrew Union College Annual,* Cincinnati, Ohio
IB	*The Interpreter's Bible,* New York and Nashville, Tenn., 1951-7
ICC	The International Critical Commentary, Edinburgh

IDB	*The Interpreter's Dictionary of the Bible*, New York and Nashville, Tenn., 1962
Interpr.	*Interpretation*, Richmond, Virginia
JBL	*Journal of Biblical Literature*, New York, etc.
KBL	L. Köhler and W. Baumgartner, *Lexicon in Veteris Testamenti Libros*, Leiden, 1953
KS	*Kleine Schriften*
LXX	The Septuagint
MT	The Massoretic text
OTL	The Old Testament Library, London
OuTWP	*Die Ou Testamentiese Werkgemeenskap in Suid-Afrika*, Pretoria
RB	*Revue Biblique*, Paris
RSV	Revised Standard Version of the Bible
SAT	*Die Schriften des Alten Testaments*, ed. H. Schmidt, Göttingen, ^{2}1923
SBT	Studies in Biblical Theology, London
SVT	*Supplements to Vetus Testamentum*, Leiden
TDNT	*Theological Dictionary of the New Testament*, ET of *ThWNT*, Grand Rapids, Mich., 1964ff.
ThB	Theologische Bücherei, München
ThLZ	*Theologische Literaturzeitung* (Leipzig), Berlin
ThWNT	*Theologisches Wörterbuch zum Neuen Testament*, ed. G. Kittel, G. Friedrich, Stuttgart, 1933ff.
UUå	Uppsala Universitets årsskrift, Uppsala and Leipzig
VT	*Vetus Testamentum*, Leiden
WMANT	Wissenschaftliche Monographien zum Alten und Neuen Testament, Neukirchen
WZ Halle	*Wissenschaftliche Zeitschrift der Martin-Luther Universität*, *Halle-Wittenburg*, Gesellschafts- und sprachwissenschaftliche Reihe
WZ Leipzig	*Wissenschaftliche Zeitschrift der Karl-Marx Universität*, *Leipzig*, Gesellschafts- und sprachwissenschaftliche Reihe
ZAW	*Zeitschrift für die Alttestamentliche Wissenschaft* (Giessen), Berlin
ZThK	*Zeitschrift für Theologie und Kirche* (Freiburg i.B., Leipzig), Tübingen

I

INTRODUCTION

During the time he was preparing his commentary on Ezekiel, in the German *Biblischer Kommentar* series,[1] Zimmerli presented a paper to the British Society for Old Testament Study entitled 'The Special Form- and Traditio-historical Character of Ezekiel's Prophecy.'[2] In it he called attention to a number of similarities between the book of Ezekiel and the so-called 'pre-classical prophetic narratives' in the books of I and II Kings. This monograph takes up those points of similarity in order to determine their significance and to give some explanation of how they arose. But a select range of other Old Testament traditions is also examined so that Ezekiel's place among Israel's prophets may be more fully appreciated.

The present chapter begins with an outline of the major changes in critical opinion during this century. Then some principles of form-critical methodology will be discussed, since comment is later called for on recent form-critical studies. Following that is a discussion of the so-called 'ecstatic' element in prophecy. The chapter concludes by describing some of the factors involved in the preservation and transmission of the prophetic narratives of I and II Kings.

A. *The course of critical opinion during this century*[3]

Ezekiel appears to be the most orderly of all prophetic books. Of its forty-eight chapters, the first half contains mainly prophecies of judgment against Jerusalem and the kingdom of Judah. The prophet is said to have spoken from exile in Babylon, some 700 miles away, where he was taken with other citizens of Jerusalem when Babylonian forces captured the city in 597 BC. The second half of the book begins with prophecies against foreign nations (chs 25–32). Then, when news of Jerusalem's destruction reaches Ezekiel, he goes on to encourage the exiles to hope for restoration to their own land (chs 33–39). In a final vision a new temple and the division of Palestine among the Israelite tribes is described (chs 40–48).

At the beginning of this century numerous textual problems and points of disorder in the book of Ezekiel had been pointed out by commentators. But the dominant view was that 'no critical question arises in connection with the authorship of the book'.⁴ In 1924, however, a study by Hölscher appeared in which Ezekiel was said to be the author of little more than one-eighth (approx. 150 verses) of the book.⁵ The basis of Hölscher's judgment was his view that Ezekiel was essentially a poet and that the majority of the prose material was from editors of the prophecy.

A few years later, Torrey tried to show that Ezekiel was a late pseudepigraph, supposedly from the time of Manasseh's reign in the seventh century, but actually originating in the third century BC.⁶ James Smith, on the other hand, believed that the corruption of Jerusalem described in Ezekiel did actually represent the evil state of affairs under Manasseh, who was ruler of the southern kingdom of Judah. The prophet, however, was said to be from the northern kingdom of Israel and it was the defeat and exile of that kingdom which he experienced in 734 BC.⁷

Another theory and one that has been widely influential, was proposed by Herntrich in 1932.⁸ In this there was a new attempt to explain Ezekiel's concern with events in Jerusalem and why many of his words are directed against its inhabitants. Herntrich divided the material between the prophet who was really active in Jerusalem (chs 1–39), and an exilic editor who reworked the genuine material, providing an exilic context and adding chs 40–48. A number of later scholars, following Herntrich's precedent, thought Ezekiel had prophesied in Jerusalem about the beginning of the sixth century BC, although they also believed he had been active among the exiles in Babylon.⁹

For all the weaknesses that are now apparent in their theories, the more extreme critics brought to attention matters which still present difficulties in the book. So it is no longer possible to regard it as a straightforward composition by a single man. Among the most important of the questions raised were: the many repetitions of phrases and, as some think, whole passages of the prophecy; the disorder of material within the unusually well-ordered framework of the book; the respective roles of poetry and prose; Ezekiel's removal from exile to Jerusalem and back by the spirit of Yahweh; and the prophet's attitude to the cult and priesthood.

There was by no means general acceptance of the views just mentioned. The major commentary of Cooke published in 1936 affirmed the traditional view of the prophet's activity.[10] But the negative views of the book's authenticity and Babylonian setting were challenged in a number of studies published between 1948 and 1952. Among the new contributions, those of Howie[11] and Fohrer[12] were most significant. Their investigations were essentially literary-critical, re-examining literary relationships and word usage, or isolating glosses within the book. The way for this had been prepared in many branches of Old Testament study. There were new archaeological findings and new developments in philology, and there had been a more sensitive assessment of the way Ezekiel understood his experiences.

The subsequent form-critical studies of Zimmerli[13] and von Rabenau[14] added significantly to understanding of the book. By identifying the forms of speech used by Ezekiel and considering their use elsewhere in the Old Testament the prophecy can be seen more clearly in the context of its time. In these, and the more recent commentaries of Eichrodt[15] and Wevers,[16] considerable attention is also paid to the way the prophet's words were re-interpreted in the course of transmission.[17]

B. *Some principles of form-critical study*

The principles of form- and traditio-historical analysis (alternatively called form-historical or literary-historical analysis) are becoming increasingly well known.[18] By sensitive appraisal of style, speech units are classified into various basic forms (or types), e.g. the dirge form, the admission torah. The forms in turn must be identified according to the situation in life (*Sitz im Leben*) – e.g. the mourning rite, the entrance liturgy – in which each had its origin and characteristic usage. Developed from the methods used by scholars investigating German folk-lore, application of these principles in Old Testament studies, through the work pioneered by Gunkel,[19] brought remarkable results. They took account of the Old Testament material's existence in oral form often for long periods. And they made possible investigation beyond the purely literary material which we now possess.

A point of special importance among form-historical principles as they were originally conceived was that forms were once rigidly determined according to function. This was true in primitive cultures as well as in ancient high civilizations. We, for example, observe particular conventions in composing commercial correspondence,[20] but stylistic conventions were far more closely adhered to by ancient peoples. There was, moreover, a more comprehensive network of forms, each characteristic of a certain task or kind of communication to be conveyed. So it was assumed that in the Old Testament we have, for the most part, to do with forms whose use was firmly defined by custom.

The advent of the Scandinavian oral-tradition school[21] strengthened interest in form-historical analysis. What Gunkel had called the 'pre-literary stage' of the forms was seen to be of greater significance. Large bodies of songs, laws, stories and prophecies were thought to have been handed down by word of mouth through the generations. The theory that various 'tradition-circles'[22] preserved such material encouraged investigation of the continuing process of transmission. Hence the term 'traditio-history'. With respect to prophecy, emphasis has shifted from attempts to distinguish 'genuine' and 'spurious' material to consideration of the continuing life of the prophets' words among their followers.

In more recent years Fohrer has expressed alarm at the proliferation of new literary types discerned, often on slender grounds, in prophetic literature.[23] And he has protested too against the assumption that any one type serves the same purpose throughout the literature in which it appears.[24] For example, the dirge in prophecy is not used to bewail actual death, but warns of or threatens destruction. Also, the use of a particular form does not necessarily link the prophet with the customary users of the form. The use by Isaiah of the love song and the form of wisdom instruction (5.1–7; 28.23–29), should not lead us to regard him as either a troubadour or a wisdom teacher.[25]

Some statements of Gunkel's have closely associated forms or types with particular classes of speakers. He regarded description of the future as the characteristic form of prophetic speech. But he also recognized that 'all manner of mixed styles are especially frequent in the prophets'.[26] Therefore we cannot assume that once we have identified the origin of a form of speech we have thereby identified the profession or office of the user. Moreover, implicit in the recognition of 'deviations and mixtures of style'[27] is acknowledgment of the need to examine the purposes of the individual user. For example, Amos employed the form of priestly instruction[28] when warning Israelites against attendance at the sanctuaries of Bethel, Gilgal and Beersheba. His cry, 'Seek me and you will live!' (5.4, cf. vv. 6, 14) directed people away from reliance upon the very institution in which 'righteousness' and 'life' were proclaimed.[29] The function or content of the form as it was currently used among Amos' contemporaries was thus altered. It demanded total commitment to goodness and justice, not mere fulfilment of the accepted standards of cultic purity.

In both the above-mentioned article and one published in German in the same year,[30] Fohrer takes a critical view also of 'tradition-history'. He points out that we must pay more attention to the successive reinterpretation of Old Testament traditions. Again he is attempting to counter those form-historical studies in which the prophets' original contributions to Israel's faith are discounted. But here we must define our terminology, for the concepts of form-historical analysis have become somewhat confused by the over-use of certain expressions. This is particularly the case with the term 'tradition-history', which has come to be used in two different ways.

The term 'traditio-history' is, as indicated above, properly used to describe the preservation and transmission of material deriving from particular persons or groups of persons, be they priestly, prophetic, courtly or lay. Thus, for example, Douglas Jones has examined the traditio of the oracles of Isaiah of Jerusalem, and the traditio of his disciples.[31] He has discerned in Isaiah 1–5 a process of reinterpretation by which Isaiah's eighth-century oracles regarding the Day of Yahweh found fresh expression in the disciples' prophecies concerning the fall of Jersualem. 'Traditio' is here used 'in its fundamental sense of delivery or giving up to another, the sense, in fact, employed by the Fathers of the Early Church'.[32] Mowinckel has, of course, shown similar appreciation of the process of preservation, development and reapplication of the traditio of the classical prophets.[21] But this he terms the develop-

ment of 'tradition', and he writes that he is concerned to determine
the 'history of tradition' within each of the various prophetic
circles. This meaning of the term 'tradition-history' (or 'traditio-
history') should, however, be distinguished from its meaning in
regard to another aspect of form-historical analysis. For the same
term is applied to the investigation of material which is common to
two or more 'tradition-circles'. It may be more appropriate to call
this feature of form-historical studies 'motif-' or 'theme-historical'
investigation. Motifs may appear in conjunction with particular
literary forms.[33] Thus Jirku identified several different summaries
of Israel's history, all presented in the same form of instruction.[34]
But we can also trace the motif of the Davidic covenant through
various narratives, prophecies and psalms. Or the motif of Yahweh's
betrothal of Israel may be traced from popular mythology through
the prophecies of Hosea, Jeremiah and Ezekiel.

It is our intention in the present study to investigate Ezekiel's
relation to prophetic tradition in the wider sense, that is, to consider the extent to which his work reflects the motifs and concepts
of other tradition circles and particularly those of the pre-classical
prophets. Nevertheless, consideration of the development of the
traditio of Ezekiel within his own circle of disciples is a necessary
part of such a study. And other points we have noted about the
principles of form- and traditio-historical analysis will also need
to be taken up later.

C. *The 'ecstatic' element in prophecy*

Another matter requiring some introductory comment is the so-
called 'ecstatic' element in prophecy, because of its importance for
understanding both Ezekiel and the pre-classical prophets.

It has been said that we have no basis for dating the beginnings
of the universal phenomenon of prophecy.[35] Here, of course,
'prophecy' is understood in the widest sense, namely as a form of
communication, by a human intermediary, of information from
powers or persons beyond the sphere of normal sense perception.
In communities as widely divergent as for example those of
Lapland and Papua New Guinea, there have been individuals who
have claimed to possess messages from spirits or from gods.
Often they have received their messages while in ecstatic states of
mind. Again, 'ecstasy' must be understood in the broadest sense.

Most frequently it denotes physical frenzy, but it may equally indicate states of passivity or trance, in which the mind sees or hears visions or auditions from the extrasensory world. Analogies in other cultures can help us understand the Israelite prophets' displays of disturbed physical and mental states. Clairvoyancy and powers of clairaudience; delivery of oracular judgments (under the influence of music or of group rituals); revelatory dreams; garbled speech, subsequently interpreted; prostration or, alternatively, spiritual transportation: such things do not characterize Old Testament prophecy alone. What does distinguish it is the way such phenomena were used to serve the purposes of Yahweh, the covenant partner of Israel.

Yet it appears that the features of 'ecstatic' behaviour just mentioned could be seen in Israel's prophets in varying degrees. In this connection, an important question, which is still the subject of controversy, is that of suitably distinguishing so-called pre-classical, reform and false prophecy. In an article published some years ago,[36] Mowinckel drew attention to the apparent lack of interest of the pre-exilic reform prophets in the dramatic demonstrations of spiritual possession which marked pre-classical prophecy. He held that violent manifestations of ecstasy became discredited as proof of inspiration. Mechanically induced prophecy (*nabi'ism*), as in I Sam. 10.5ff., was associated with false spirits (I Kings 22.22). From the time of Amos the reform prophets spurned such claims and demonstrations of their callings and reverted to the forms of the old seers, who had their messages whispered – (*ne'um*) – to them, or saw visions in the night. They claimed to bear the 'word' of Yahweh, not his 'spirit'. Only in Ezekiel do we find again a true ecstatic of the old type, although of course Ezekiel shares the moral and religious earnestness of the reformers.

There is some justification for this view. The spirit's association with more violent forms of prophetic activity is undeniable (cf. I Sam.19.20ff.). And the spirit is not referred to frequently by the pre-exilic reform prophets. But it would be a grave mistake to distinguish firmly between pre-classical and reform prophets on the basis of ecstatic behaviour. On the one hand, biographical interest is strictly limited in the Old Testament, so that, as Porteous says, 'it is a mistake to assume *a priori* that the experience of the great prophets is directly accessible to modern psychological methods'.[37]

On the other hand, Skinner warns us against 'an absolute breach of continuity [in the great prophets] with the kind of experience which was admittedly characteristic of the earlier *nabi'ism*'.[38] Unusual traits of mind and behaviour are certainly in evidence among the classical prophets with their visions and acted prophecies (e.g. Amos 7.1ff.; Isa. 20.1ff.). Moreover, the sphere of the divine played an incomparably more significant role in the thinking of ancient man that it does in ours. Such manifestations of divine power and knowledge of the divine will were not necessarily signs of sickness or mental instability. Rather, giving due weight to historical and psychological perspectives, they were evidence of prophetic vocations and were appropriate means of fulfilling those vocations.

It should be emphasized that ecstatic experience is not an essential characteristic of Israelite prophecy. The Elohist implies Abraham was a prophet by virtue of his role as an intercessor (Gen. 20.7). Despite such passages as II Samuel 7.4, in which the word of Yahweh comes in a vision of the night, Nathan is cast more in the role of a counsellor of extraordinary perception and moral rectitude, than in that of a possessed gabbler of divine mysteries. Exodus 4.15f. and 7.1 call Aaron a prophet because he acted as the spokesman of Moses. To quote Rowley, prophecy 'is concerned with the essence, not the form of inspiration, and what it here has quite clearly in mind is one who delivers a message not his own, and not one who falls into a fit'.[39] Yet it is in features of the external form of inspiration – of transportation under the influence of the spirit, of prostration and loss of speech, etc. – that Ezekiel bears striking resemblance to pre-classical prophets. And this similarity of ecstatic tradition helps explain the unusual character of Ezekiel's prophetic experience.

D. *The prophetic narratives of I and II Kings*

Detailed consideration is given in the next chapter to a number of ways in which Ezekiel's prophecy reflects concepts, manners of expression and literary forms found elsewhere largely in the pre-classical prophetic traditions recorded in I and II Kings. There are two fundamental ways in which Ezekiel's work could have been influenced by pre-classical prophecy. The first is that of simple literary dependence on the records of his predecessors. The second is that pre-classical concepts continued to be used by some groups of prophets. Approximately 250 years separated the periods of activity of Elijah and Ezekiel, so that the relationship we shall be examining raises the important question of how prophetic tradition was preserved.

The narratives of I Kings 17–II Kings 10 are, in their written form, of north Israelite origin. This is confirmed by a number of linguistic peculiarities that are also found in northern narratives of Judges and Samuel,[40] and by the early influence of Aramaic.[41]

Division of the material according to whether or not it is likely to be historical reveals a considerable portion which was probably compiled soon after the events related. The graphic, though restrained, character of these narratives suggests we have in them extracts from a history of the reigns of Ahab, Jehoram and Jehu.[42] The atmosphere of Syrian oppression indicates that this material was completed early in the eighth century BC, soon after the death of Elisha, but before the wars of Jeroboam II. It is the product of learned minds and is commonly attributed to the upper class of Israelite society.[43]

A second kind of material is found in the stories directly concerned with the persons of Elijah and Elisha, describing their involvement in the political, social and more specifically religious events of their days. These narratives[44] may rest on a genuine historical basis and doubtless reflect real opposition, on the part of those prophets, toward the house of Omri on account of its encouragement of Baal worship. Šanda, and subsequently John Gray, consider the saga cycle involving Elijah derived its basic character from Elisha himself; the restraint with which miracle is appealed to, and the exercise of the prophet's powers in the service of wider national and religious purposes, is in marked contrast to the third class of material composing the northern narratives, in which miracles serve largely to demonstrate the prophets' superhuman capabilities. They are fed by marvellous means, may call down fire or evoke other natural calamities on their enemies, raise the dead, cause iron to float, etc. Interest in the prophets themselves dominates the narratives and the events related are of a trivial nature. This suggests to Gray that the third kind of material derived from the dervish orders, to which the expression 'sons of the prophets' refers. Those circles, at various shrines associated with Elisha, possibly competed with one another in the local miracles which they related of the prophet. The features of lively dialogue, verbal repetition and dramatic suspense to stimulate interest, indicate there was a considerable period of oral transmission and development of these traditions.[45]

The reference of I Kings 19.15–17 to the anointing of Hazael as king of Syria indicates a date of composition for the more historical traditions concerning Elijah (I Kings 18–19, 21) not later than 825 BC. For Hazael's attack on Jehu at that time proved him to be no ally of Israel. Even at this early stage, if the literary unity of chs 17–19 is accepted,[46] a legendary element has been added (in ch. 17) to the more historical traditions. Firm grounds for dating the remaining portions of the saga cycles are lacking, but it is reasonable to expect stories of supernatural activities to be associated with such outstanding charismatic figures even during their lifetimes.[47] Thus there is no need to reject Šanda's suggestion of a date of literary composition about 790–780 BC for the stories of Elisha circulating among 'the sons of the prophets'.[48] The influence of Aramaic in some parts of the more historical stories concerning Elisha[49] implies that they were composed at a later period.

Even if the above dates are considered rather early for the corresponding material to have been written down, it is clear that the northern narratives of I Kings 17ff. attained basically their present character before the sack of Samaria and the collapse of the northern kingdom in 721 BC. Only so can the awareness of the distinction between the two kingdoms of Israel, the peculiarities of style already referred to, and the acute awareness of the pressures of various enemies on Israel's borders, be adequately explained. Moreover, it is not intended to minimize the lapse of time between the compilation of the northern prophetic material in the books of Kings and the recurrence of the various concepts, characteristic of it, in Ezekiel. The pre-classical prophetic concepts which recur in Ezekiel are found not only in the marvellous tales told of the prophet leaders, but in the history of the kings, which includes the earliest of the material.

Montgomery has attributed the composition of the northern narratives of Kings to members of prophetic guilds.[50] But in that case, it is surprising that we have no collections of prophetic 'words' such as we find predominating in the canonical prophecies, even from such a short time later in Amos. We have instead only sayings of such a character as could have been invented by narrators to suit the events described. While collections of authentic prophecies may have been made,[51] and the present dialogue undoubtedly reflects prophetic speech forms current in the authors' period, we cannot affirm that the accounts we now have of these prophets' activities contain the actual words of the prophets concerned.[52] Indeed, their dissimilarity from canonical prophecy and their setting within a broader context of historical narrative suggest we should seek their authors within a larger circle of individuals, whose concern was to preserve a wider range of Israelite tradition, and whose literary ability – in a time when 'a knowledge of writing was probably a rare accomplishment'[53] – is less questionable.

The identity of such a circle is suggested by one of Wolff's studies in Hosea,[54] where he has drawn attention to evidence of an alliance between prophets and Levites in northern Israel. Despite the unfaithfulness of the people, priests and some prophets,[55] Hosea believed that he represented a stream of prophetic tradition rooted in the activity of Moses (12.13). And he also displays knowledge of traditions which are most likely to have been transmitted by Levites. These concern opposition to the cult at Bethel[56] and reflect traditions recorded elsewhere of intense Levitical zeal for the Sinai-Horeb covenant in the face of the people's apostasy.[57]

A similar combination of prophetic and Levitical interests is apparent in Deuteronomy, whose close affinities to Hosea[58] are perhaps best typified by the exclusive love relationship they envisage existing ideally between Yahweh and Israel. Deuteronomy portrays Moses as a prophet (18.15–18). But that should not be taken to indicate that Deuteronomy was composed by prophets rather than Levites.[59] Due weight must be given to the persistent urging of charity toward country Levites in the primary material of the code. And in later additions there is material supporting Levitical claims to the Israelite priesthood.[60] The Levitical traditions of the Old Testament are extremely complex, but those Levites who served as priests at Israelite sanctuaries would, like other priests, have contributed significantly to recording and preserving Israelite tradition. For sanctuaries were 'the place of written tradition'[61] and the hereditary nature of the priesthood ensured continuity of tradition.[62]

Although Deuteronomy was composed with the reform of the

Jerusalem cult in mind,[63] the northern origin of a number of the traditions which underlie it is now widely recognized.[64] Also, the rest of the Deuteronomic history (Joshua to II Kings) betrays sympathy toward both Levitical concerns (e.g. I Kings 12.25–33) and prophetic activity, as well as broader interest in Israel's institutions. So the inclusion of the northern pre-classical prophetic narratives of Kings within the Deuteronomic history suggests that the narratives were initially recorded and preserved among the opposition group of Levites and prophets in northern Israel and brought south by refugees after 721 BC.

It is also important to note that Hosea's prophecy, features of which, as we shall see, appear to be reflected in Ezekiel, was also preserved and brought south. There it had an impact of fundamental importance on Jeremiah, who, like Hosea, though by virtue of his descent from the priests of Anathoth, may have been associated with a Levitical group.[65]

There is ample evidence in the Old Testament to indicate that ordinary Israelites (or more specifically 'the elders of Israel') were responsible for the instruction of their families in the traditions of their people. And as we shall point out, it is to these individuals, in part, that we must look in identifying those who preserved Ezekiel's prophecies. Yet indications of the special responsibilities the Levites were aware of as the zealous advocates of the Sinai/Horeb covenant, and evidence of their interest in preserving prophetic tradition in the Deuteronomic history, suggest that Levites have contributed greatly to the continuity of prophetic tradition in Israel.

II

EZEKIEL AND PRE-CLASSICAL PROPHECY

Various similarities between Ezekiel and the pre-classical prophets must now be examined.

A. *The hand of Yahweh*

In Ezekiel, the phrase 'the hand of Yahweh was upon me' (*hāyᵉtā* [*wattᵉhī*] *'ālay yad-yhwh*) is found seven times with little variation in the manner of expression.[1] The phrase is in first person style except in Ezekiel 1.3b where it appears to have been altered to agree with the third person style at the beginning of the verse. The primary sense of the word *yad* is 'hand' but it is often used in the figurative sense of 'power'. Joseph had at his disposal Potiphar's property. Therefore he said, 'my master . . . has given all that he has into my hand' (Gen. 39.8). Israel is to be delivered from the oppressive 'hand of the Egyptians' (Ex. 3.8). And we hear of lands or people being given 'into the hand' of Israel (as in Josh. 2.24). The symbolic laying on of hands was important in acts of blessing (Gen. 48.14) and of sacrifice (Lev. 4.3f, 15). At the commissioning of Joshua the laying of Moses' hand on the younger man signified the transfer of authority (Num. 27.18, 23).

Zimmerli[2] has suggested that the Exodus tradition was the source of Old Testament interest in 'the hand of Yahweh'. The image satisfactorily described Yahweh's means of action in the world. The Deuteronomists frequently refer to the 'mighty hand and outstretched arm' of Yahweh as the means of deliverance from Egypt (Deut. 4.34 etc.).[3] And the wide acceptance of the image is shown by its continued use in post-exilic material. These later writings refer to 'the hand of Yahweh' to explain success in human endeavours. 'The (good) hand of Yahweh (their) God was upon (them)', i.e. upon Ezra, Nehemiah and the returning Jews (Ezra 7.6, 9, 28; 8.18; etc.; Neh. 2.8, 18). In pre-exilic prophecy, however, allusions to 'the hand of Yahweh' are found more in passages concerning divine judgment against Israel (Isa. 5.25; Amos 9.2). Ezekiel also betrays knowledge of the 'mighty hand and outstretched arm' characteristic of the Deuteronomic references to the Exodus (Ezek. 20.33ff.). But his interest, like Isaiah's and Amos', was mainly in the work of purifying and punishing that Yahweh's hand would accomplish among his chosen people (6.14; 16.27; etc.), and among their neighbours (25.7, 13, etc.).

Such passages as we have just quoted from the prophets, however, throw clearly into relief the references to 'the hand of Yahweh' upon Ezekiel which were mentioned at the beginning of this section.[1] To understand them we need to examine two passages in Kings (I Kings 18.46; II Kings 3.15), one in Isaiah (8.11) and one in Jeremiah (15.17). All refer to a prophet's awareness of the presence of 'the hand of Yahweh' upon him.

I Kings 18.46: This verse tells of Elijah running from Carmel to Jezreel before the chariot of Ahab, when the hand of Yahweh came upon him. The phrase 'and the hand of Yahweh was upon Elijah' (*weyad-yhwh hāyetā 'el-ēlīyyāhū*) is very similar to the expression we have noted in Ezekiel. Allowing of course for the transition to the third person style, the only difference is the use of *'el-* for the expected *'al-*. But this simple variation in spelling is very widespread and occurs even within the book of Ezekiel.[4] Elijah's action did not necessarily require superhuman power despite Zimmerli's description of it as 'an inconceivable feat of strength'.[5] He 'ran' before the king's chariot but so did those other individuals who served as the king's escorts (I Sam. 8.11), presumably to secure the king from attack.[6] Absalom had fifty such escorts (II Sam. 15.1), as did Adonijah (I Kings 1.5). These same 'runners' may have been identical with the royal bodyguard referred to in I Sam. 22.17; I Kings 14.27f.; etc.

There was another sort of 'runner', however. Such was the messenger delivering news of Absalom's death (II Sam. 18.19ff.) or the outcome of battle (Jer. 51.31). Speed, stamina and ability to cope with the obstacles which rough terrain might present, would have been essential qualities of those men. But that the royal

chariotry was accompanied by foot-guards, and could even have
been preceded by messengers on foot, indicates the need for care in
interpreting I Kings 18.46. Elijah's journey of some seventeen
miles, from Carmel to Jezreel, ahead of Ahab, may reveal only the
physical condition of the prophet. It was a feat requiring stamina,
but did not necessarily require supernatural aid. It is reported, by a
student of Arabic customs, that messengers on foot can cover 100
miles of desert road in less than two days.[7] Moreover, if we accept
the tradition of the three-year drought (I Kings 17.1ff.), 'the
earth would be gashed with great cracks and the sudden flush of
rain (I Kings 18.45) down the dry watercourses would impose
further obstacles [on chariotry], to say nothing of the mud'.[8] Gray
also reminds us that in this same region, the greater mobility of
the pedestrian Israelites aided in the rout and pursuit of the
chariotry of Sisera (Judg. 4.12–16).

Divine intervention was not necessary for Elijah to run from
Carmel to Jezreel before the king. Thus we cannot, from the
physical demands of the journey, conclude that the coming of 'the
hand of Yahweh' implies the imparting of superhuman powers.
But we are justified in emphasizing the connection of 'the hand'
with movement from place to place. This is especially clear if the
imperfect consecutives of the phrase 'and he girded up his loins
and ran' (*way^ešannēs māt^enāw wayyārāṣ*) have the sense of logical or
necessary consequence.[9] Movement from place to place, even by
the individual's own physical powers, may have been implied
when 'the hand of Yahweh' came upon a man.

Yet looking beyond the physical demands of the journey, the
reference to Yahweh's hand on the prophet suggests that the
journey was later thought to have been divinely empowered. This
would have been consistent with Elijah's general manner of life.
For he was a 'man of God' who could bring life (I Kings 17.22) or
death (II Kings 1.17), produce food (I Kings 17.14) and rain (I
Kings 18.42ff.), and even make 'fire' fall from heaven (I Kings
18.38). These deeds constituted Elijah's prophetic credentials. On
account of them the widow of Zarephath said: 'Now I know that
you are a man of God and the word of Yahweh is really in your
mouth'[10] (I Kings 17.24). So it would not have been surprising if
one who participated in the work of Yahweh so fully had been
granted supernatural means of conveyance. Elijah was, after all,
translated to heaven by a fiery chariot (II Kings 2.11). Also,

Obadiah, Ahab's chamberlain, feared that 'the spirit of Yahweh' would carry Elijah away so that he could not be found (I Kings 18.12). Of itself, this passage may be thought of as just a dramatic explanation for Elijah hiding himself. Read in conjunction with II Kings 2.16, however, it indicates that Elijah was believed to be subject to actual physical removal from place to place, by the spirit of Yahweh. This second passage concerns a prophetic brotherhood's request of Elisha that they might search for Elijah in the mountains and valleys after his translation to heaven. The same verb is used of the spirit's activity in I Kings 18.12 and II Kings 2.16 (as also in Ezek.3.12, 14; 8.3; 11.1, 24; 43.5). The spirit 'lifts, bears or takes away' (*nśʾ*) the prophet. Similar experiences are reported of Philip (Acts 8.39) and by Paul (II Cor.12.2) in the New Testament, although in these examples, the verb ἁρπάζω[11] suggests more the extraordinary nature of the experience. It was a case of being 'torn, or carried away by force', by a power which acted independently of the subject's own will.[12] But it may be inferred, from Elijah's assurance to Obadiah that he would meet Ahab (I Kings 18.15), that the prophet was able to exercise at least some control in the matter of removal by the spirit.

We need not consider the various explanations of these and similar events at this point.[13] Whether they are judged to be hallucinations or not; whether they are said to have involved physical translocation or not, depends on the presuppositions of the interpreter. What is significant is that in Elijah we have an individual who was believed to be subject to translocation by the aid of Yahweh's spirit.

To summarize the above: it seems likely that at some stage of its transmission the account of Elijah's journey to Jezreel was understood as a feat accomplished with the assistance of Yahweh. It is true that there has been no attempt to narrate the journey specifically in terms of translocation by the spirit: 'the spirit of Yahweh bore him . . .' (*nᵉśāʾō rūaḥ yhwh*). But what may originally have been a mundane, if strenuous, act of the prophet has been reported in a way that implies that Yahweh was active on the prophet's behalf. Mention of 'the hand of Yahweh' upon Elijah was thus associated with his movement from place to place and was probably intended to imply the granting to him of power and endurance greater than that of normal men.

II Kings 3.15: Here a technique for obtaining revelation is described. The verse is part of a speech of Elisha in which he requests that a minstrel be brought to him, 'for it used to happen (*weḥāyā*) when the minstrel played that the hand of Yahweh came upon him'. It seems that this was no rare event. The word *weḥāyā* is best understood to mean that the action had been repeated more or less frequently in the past.[14] So II Kings 3.15 tells not merely of one instance in which a prophet was aided by music, but indicates that this was a regular occurrence. The purpose of the minstrel's playing is seen in the following verses. When 'the hand of Yahweh' came upon Elisha he uttered oracles. And this he could apparently do upon request, given the assistance of a musician.

Many examples of the influence of music (and dancing) on the human mind have been recorded in recent years. Such observations have by no means been restricted to the rituals of so-called 'primitive' people. Modern Western cultures offer numerous examples of the use of aural stimuli for political, religious and commercial ends.[15] Attempts to go beyond the mere description of observable phenomena (such as rhythmic music, dancing or speaking, and the visible or audible responses), to consider the mental processes involved, remain tentative. Philosophers have long discussed alternative theories of the mind-body relationship[16] and neurophysiologists readily acknowledge their limited understanding of brain functions.[17] Yet it does appear that 'there is a causative relation between material and psychical reality, that the psychic states depend on cerebral processes, and the latter in turn on physical stimuli'.[18] Further, man appears to have a distinct affinity to rhythmic sound and his mental activity may be deeply affected by it. For example, the same student who finds help in concentrating by a background sound of classical music may be stimulated to seeming hysteria by a College band at a football match. Neurophysiologists explain this by the correlation of external patterns of sound or movement and the patterns of electrical charge or discharge within the brain. The brain is thought to consist of a vast aggregation of electrical cells whose charges alternate with varying frequency and force.[19]

The first Old Testament passage directly associating music with the attainment of a state susceptible to inspiration is I Sam. 10.1ff. In I Sam. 10.5-6 Samuel foretells the meeting between Saul and a band of prophets, who prophesy to the accompaniment of harp, tambourine, flute and lyre. Saul is caught up by the enthusiasm of the group and prophesies with them (v. 10). Indeed, when the spirit of the Lord comes upon him he is 'turned into another man'. This reinforces the observation already made that external stimuli such as music may be associated with changes in a person's behaviour. These changes may be quite marked and may be temporary or permanent.[20]

Again, the presence of a spirit from the Lord is associated with music in I Sam. 16.14ff. An evil spirit, apparently manifest in Saul's periods of depression, was dispelled by David's lyre playing (v. 23). But the therapeutic effect of music[21] seems to have had less impact at a later stage (I Sam. 18.10; 19.9). Even while David played, the 'evil spirit' overwhelmed Saul and he attempted to take David's life, although here the motive of jealousy dominates the narrative.

A point to note is that the repetitive and emotional character of traditional Oriental melody patterns[22] could apparently influence men's subconscious drives, even without the strong rhythmic emphasis provided by the tambourines and cymbals which are said to have been used in the episode of I Samuel 10.5ff. For David played before Saul on a harp or lyre (I Sam. 16.23) and the verb used to describe his activity – (*ngn*, piel) – is also found in II Kings 3.15. It was evidently to stringed instruments that Elisha listened when 'the hand of Yahweh came upon him'.

It should not surprise us that the strange activities of prophets (cf. I Sam. 19.24; II Kings 9.11) were attributed to beings or powers working through the disturbed individuals. The attempts of men to explain forces beyond their control or understanding by the influence of (good or evil) spirits persist to the present day.[23] Behind the association of music with the activity of spirits lies a long history of music's magical connotations in the primitive mind.[24] Traces of this can still be discerned in the Old Testament,[25] but Ambros has noted Israel's distinctive conception of music's relation to life:

> In the case of the Hebrews, the miraculous effects of music as described in most of the sagas and myths of the peoples of antiquity acquired a theosophical character. . . . Hebrew music was a *musica sacra*, a bridge linking humanity to the spiritual world that is above nature; it was the bearer of prayer, and, as a gracious return gift, it brought from the God of Abraham, Isaac and Jacob prophetic

illumination, a benediction on the land and its fruits, miraculous victory over the enemy, . . . not aesthetics but religion determined its value.[26]

To summarize: the use of music to obtain divine revelations implies that such revelations were received while the prophet was in a special state of mind. Whether the effect of the music was to sooth or stimulate him, II Kings 3.15 indicates that 'the hand of Yahweh' came upon Elisha on specific occasions which the prophet could arrange. And in that special condition of mind he was made aware of Yahweh's will concerning selected matters.

Jeremiah 15.17: Jeremiah 15.10–11, 15–18 belongs to the so-called 'confessions' of the prophet and may be understood as a personal complaint about the hardship he faces.[27] Jeremiah's grief is so intense that he loathes his very life: 'Woe to me, my mother, that you bore me; a man of strife and contention to the whole land' (v. 10). The reason for this outburst is not only the sensitive character of the prophet himself,[28] but the nature of his task as it is described in ch. 16. He is denied the companionship of a wife and family (16.2). He is forbidden to sympathize with his fellow-men in their afflictions (16.5ff.). His solitary existence precludes participation in the pleasures and celebrations of the people (16.8). This burden of profound isolation is reflected in Jer. 15.17: 'I did not sit in the company of merry-makers, nor did I rejoice; *because of your hand, I sat alone*' (*mippᵉnē yādᵉkā bādād yāšabtī*).

The parallel expressions – 'merry-making' ‖ 'rejoicing' – in Jer. 15.17 together indicate that a whole range of joyful emotions, of both a profane and religious character, were in the prophet's mind. Both pleasure at human success and community well-being, and joy in the community's sense of the presence and protection of Yahweh were denied the prophet. Such was the burden of one appointed, even before his birth, as a prophet to the nations (1.5), to convey the words of Yahweh to his people (1.9; 15.16). There is no reference here to physical activity on the part of the prophet. Nor is 'the hand' connected with special moments of divine revelation, or an extraordinary state of mind. Whether 'with' or 'upon' him, Yahweh's hand marked Jeremiah out as a man apart. He was to manifest in his own life the imminent isolation and grief of those who had deserted Yahweh.

Here 'the hand of Yahweh' signifies a prophet's calling.[29]

There is an analogy in the account of Joshua's commissioning, when Moses laid his hand on Joshua (Num. 27.18ff.).[30] But in contrast to the prophetic narratives of Kings, there is a distinct widening of the concept of 'the hand of Yahweh' in relation to prophetic existence. Instead of marking particular moments in a prophet's life, 'the hand of Yahweh' may signify a prophet's life-long responsibility[31] for conveying by word and deed Yahweh's will to his people.

Isaiah 8.11: The fourth passage which is often related to Ezekiel's 'hand of Yahweh' motif is Isa. 8.11. The verse may be rendered: 'For thus said Yahweh to me, *with strength (or, force)*[32] *of the hand* (*beḥezqat hayyād*), and warned me not to walk[33] in the way of this people, saying . . .'.

One cannot, without unwarrantedly supplementing the text, translate the phrase *beḥezqat hayyād* as the RSV does: 'with (Yahweh's) strong hand upon me'. There is no evidence to support the interpolation of *'ālay* ('upon me'). To make the expression agree with that found in Ezekiel and Kings ('the hand of Yahweh was upon me'), is to ignore the possibility of important differences of usage. Both Duhm and G. B. Gray have interpreted the text in the light of Ezekiel's experience of 'the hand' upon him.[34] But there are in fact two ways in which *beḥezqat hayyād* may be understood. The first is that it may simply indicate that the message of Isa. 8.11–15 came to the prophet with unusual force. The second is to regard it as indeed an allusion to the complex of ideas associated with 'the hand of Yahweh', which we have been examining in Kings and Jeremiah. These alternatives need to be examined in turn.

(i) We have already noticed the close association of the word 'hand' with the concept of power. At the conclusion of the narrative of Moses' first meeting with Pharaoh (Ex. 5.1–6.1) the Yahwist has the Lord say to Moses: 'Now you will see what I will do to Pharaoh, for[35] *with a strong hand* (*beyād ḥazāqā*) he will drive (thy people) out of his land' (Ex. 6.1). Here is an early use of a derivative of the root *ḥzq* 'to be strong' (viz. the adjective *ḥāzāq*), with the word 'hand' to signify an activity executed 'powerfully'. Noth, in fact, renders *beyād ḥazāqā* in Ex. 6.1 as 'by force' or 'forcibly'.[36] The Deuteronomists later made frequent allusion to the role of the strong hand of Yahweh in the Exodus events,[37] but the early description of powerful acts by the imagery of 'strong hands' in Ex. 6.1 must be given due weight in the interpretation of Isa. 8.11.

R. B. Y. Scott has rendered *beḥezqat hayyād* as 'with compelling power'.[38] That Yahweh's word could be experienced as an overwhelming, compulsive force is clear from Amos 3.8: 'The Lord God has spoken, who can but prophesy?'[39] (and cf. 7.14–15). If we may ascribe to Isaiah's message in 8.12–15 the importance Scott attributes to it, the unusual stress on the urgency of the revelation in the introductory verse 11 is understandable. Scott says of vv. 12–15:

> This is apparently the first summons to men in the history of biblical religion to separate themselves in spirit from their social group in obedience to God. It was a moment pregnant with significance for the future histories of Judaism and of the Christian church.[40]

Thus *beḥezqat hayyād* may be no more than an old and widely used idiom for an intense experience.

(ii) 'The hand' of Yahweh in Isa. 8.11 clearly does not relate to any translocation of the prophet, as in the case of Elijah. Also, the reception of revelation is adequately indicated by 'thus said Yahweh to me' (Isa. 8.11a).[41] But if 'the hand of Yahweh' was widely associated in prophetic circles with the reception of revelation, as it was in the case of Elisha, *beḥezqat hayyād* may simply reinforce the claim for the divine origin of this particular message. Moreover, Scott's reference to the impending isolation of the prophet on account of the nature of the message (vv. 12–15) calls to mind the context of Jeremiah's reference to 'the hand' of Yahweh. It was because of Yahweh's hand that Jeremiah was cut off from the common life of his people. 'The hand' in Isaiah 8.11 may then be an allusion to the special responsibility of the prophet's vocation, which Isaiah felt with great intensity at this moment of impending separation from normal community aspirations.

There is nothing in Isa. 8.11 to imply that the revelation was derived after the fashion of Elisha, i.e. in a state of mind induced by music or other forms of artificial stimulation. Yet if 'the hand' is in fact to be understood here as signifying the reception of divine revelation, it does not appear to denote a life-long prophetic commission, as in Jer. 15.17. 'The hand' is with or upon the prophet specifically at the moment of revelation.

To summarize: Isa. 8.11 does not offer conclusive evidence that Isaiah understood 'the hand of Yahweh' in the manner of Jeremiah and those who preserved the prophetic narratives of Kings. The possibility that he did so understand the concept remains an open one. But the reference to Yahweh's hand here may simply indicate an intensely felt experience.

We must now consider, in the light of the above, the manner in which 'the hand of Yahweh' motif is used in describing Ezekiel's prophetic experience. There are a number of important similarities between Ezekiel and Kings:

(i) The most clearly evident is the remarkable correspondence of expression: 'the hand of Yahweh was upon him/me' (*hāyᵉtā ʿālāw/ ʿālay yad-yhwh*). It is true that there are a number of minor variations in Ezekiel, but the recurrence of the basic phrase in the prophetic narratives of Kings suggests the possibility of a literary relationship existing between the two works.

(ii) Jeremiah 15.17 indicates that a prophet could refer to 'the hand of the Lord' to signify his continuing responsibility before God. In Ezekiel, however, 'the hand' upon the prophet distinguishes certain episodes in his life and is not a constant feature of his prophetic experience. For Ezekiel, as for Elijah and Elisha (and possibly Isaiah), 'the hand of Yahweh' comes at particular times, which are so clearly distinguishable from other periods that they may even be fully dated (Ezek. 1.3; 8.1; 40.1).

(iii) It has been pointed out that II Kings 3.15 implies Elisha was in some way removed from his normal conscious state when he felt 'the hand of Yahweh' upon him. Ezekiel makes no mention of music as an aid to inspiration, but if his prophecy, in the form we now have it, is at all a reliable record of his experiences, it is clear that he too knew some alienation from normal conscious perception. We shall have more to say of this when we consider his references to 'the spirit (of Yahweh)'. For the present, it is enough to point out that 'the hand of Yahweh' is associated with 'visions' in 1.3; 3.22; 8.1; 37.1; 40.1. Both Elisha and Ezekiel (and again, perhaps Isaiah also) were made to understand things beyond normal human perception when 'the hand of Yahweh' came upon them.

(iv) Elijah's translocation when 'the hand' comes upon him is also paralleled in Ezekiel. Again, fuller consideration is given this matter in the following section. But removal of Ezekiel from place to place is connected with 'the hand' in 3.14; 3.22; 8.1; 37.1; 40.1. In 3.22f. ('and I rose and went forth into the plain'), Ezekiel implies that physical effort on his own part was involved in the journey. In the same way, Elijah was said to have 'girded up his loins and run' with the hand of Yahweh upon him.

These points of similarity between the experiences of Ezekiel and the pre-classical prophets indicate a community of shared ideas, the range of which will be seen to be even wider. But references to 'the hand of Yahweh' outside Ezekiel and Kings warn against assuming that an exclusive relationship existed between these prophetic traditions.

Before considering the role of 'the spirit' in Ezekiel, mention should be made of one further passage linking 'the hand of Yahweh' with the physical and mental capacities of the prophet. Ezekiel 33.22 refers to the alleviation of the prophet's dumbness. When 'the hand' came upon him he was able to speak again. Here there are further implications which need to be accounted for in considering Ezekiel's mental constitution and the influence of this on his prophetic activity.

B. *The concept of the spirit*

The spirit is frequently referred to in Ezekiel. It is 'the spirit' which animates the 'living creatures' of the opening vision.[42] 'Spirit' provides physical power for Ezekiel to stand upright, after lying prostrate before the awesome vision of divine glory,[43] and 'the spirit (of Yahweh)' is involved in the prophecies of restoration.[44] But the most striking references are to 'spirit' or 'a spirit' lifting the prophet up and leading him about in visionary experiences.[45] To understand Ezekiel at this point we need first to investigate the wider significance of the spirit on Israelite life and in prophecy generally.

(i) *The wider significance of the spirit*
Sometimes 'the spirit of Yahweh' has been associated so closely with prophecy that other aspects of its activity have been neglected. The foresight and administrative gifts of Joseph (Gen.

41.38), the impulse to action of the judges (Judg. 3.10 et al.) and the unparalleled leadership of king David (I Sam. 16.13) were all attributed to 'the spirit' which came upon them. Even the authority of the elders was established by the spirit's activity reported in Num. 11.17, 24–30. Thus a considerable variety of men are said to have stood in that special relationship to Yahweh which was signified by possession of his spirit. An attribute common to them all, however, was that they were leaders of men, zealous for Yahweh and bearing special responsibility for accomplishing his will, whether by acts of just administration, military leadership or personal physical prowess. It is not surprising that certain prophets were explicitly included in this group. Among the prophets 'the charismatic side of Yahwism came to expression with a completely new force'. [46] But nor is it surprising that prophecy was characterized by other more distinctive attributes than possession of the spirit.

There are remarkably few references to 'the spirit of Yahweh' in pre-exilic canonical prophecy. Amos, Zephaniah, Nahum and Jeremiah never mention the spirit or link their work with its operation. Isaiah too does not connect the spirit with his prophetic activity. Only in Hosea and Micah, and possibly in Habakkuk, are there traces of such a connection.

As we have noted in the previous chapter, Mowinckel believes that the virtual absence of allusions to 'the spirit' in pre-exilic canonical prophecy is to be explained by reference to the so-called 'false prophets'. [47] He considers that the use of ecstatic techniques and the demonstration of spiritual possession by prophets with no true concern for Israel's well-being (e.g. Micah 3.5; Jer. 23) led the canonical prophets to turn from appeals to 'the spirit' as the source of inspiration. Instead, revelatory experiences were alluded to simply in such terms as 'Yahweh said to me,' 'the word of Yahweh came to me', etc. That is to say, the pre-exilic canonical prophets appealed to 'the word' rather than to 'the spirit' of Yahweh in order to validate their pronouncements.

In discussing the prophetic narratives of I Kings 17ff., von Rad states that 'the presence of "the spirit of Yahweh" was absolutely constitutive' for prophecy in the ninth century. [48] But as we have just noted, possession of the spirit was not the exclusive prerogative of prophets, nor were claims to its possession made on behalf of such figures as Nathan, Ahijah (I Kings 11; 14), the prophets of Judah and Bethel (I Kings 13) or Jehu (I Kings 16). On the other hand, the pre-classical prophets were just as concerned as the later reform prophets to emphasize that they had heard the word of Yahweh. So, for example, did Samuel (I Sam. 15.1), Zedekiah (I Kings 22.11), Elijah (I Kings 17.8) and Elisha (II Kings 2.21). Furthermore, the prophets of David's court, Gad (I Sam. 22.5) and Nathan (II Sam. 7.2ff.), and the prophets of whom we read in I Kings 11ff., do not mention Yahweh's spirit, but are concerned to communicate Yahweh's word. It cannot be argued from this that the prophets referred to did not claim to possess the spirit of Yahweh. But it appears that from an early date such claims were not felt to be of primary importance in vindicating the prophets' rights to speak as inspired bearers of divine revelation.

Kaufmann has rightly emphasized that 'the word' rather than 'the spirit' was 'the primary source of prophecy'. The effects of the spirit may have been adjuncts of prophecy, but the revelation of the will of God was not necessarily bound up with the action of the spirit.[49] It was only in late traditions that the spirit was regarded as a general power of prophetic inspiration in ancient times.[50] But this view partly depended on the post-exilic idea that God was remote from the sphere of earthly things, and required some such vehicle of mediation for the exercise of power in it.[51]

There are only two instances, in what may properly be regarded as prophetic contexts, in which it is clearly indicated that the spirit imparts revelations. The first is found in I Kings 22.23, where Micaiah tells of the lying spirit in the mouths of the prophets who are to entice Ahab to his doom. The second occurs in Ezek. 11.5: 'The spirit of Yahweh fell upon me, and he said to me, "Say, thus says Yahweh . . ."'. It is of interest that this parallel to I Kings 22.23 appears in Ezekiel, but it is unlikely to be part of the primary material of the prophecy. It is 'the hand of Yahweh' not his 'spirit' that 'falls' or 'comes' upon the prophet elsewhere (1.3 etc.). Ezekiel 11.1 indicates that the prophet was already aware of the spirit's influence in his experience in quite a different way. And other commands to prophesy similar to 11.4 (34.2; 37.4, 9) make no reference to the spirit communicating the content of the prophecy. Zimmerli regards the phrase as 'a clumsy addition of a disciple'.[52]

A. R. Johnson has described 'the spirit of Yahweh' as an 'extension' of the divine personality.[53] But there seems to be more emphasis in pre-exilic traditions on 'the spirit' bestowing physical vitality[54] than on it communicating knowledge of the divine will. Even in I Kings 22, the primary importance of the divine 'word' in prophetic experience is indicated. For the spirit's deceitful intent was recognized by Micaiah because of the oral proceedings of the divine council, presided over by Yahweh. Also, the reference which Humbert sees in Hab. 1.11 to the 'spirit' leaving the prophet at the end of a revelatory experience – 'then *rūaḥ* passed by and was gone' – does not imply that the spirit conveyed the message to the prophet. Rather, the presence of the spirit indicates the special state of mind, or even physical condition of the prophet, at the time he received the revelation.[55]

Buber distinguished the prophetic 'spirit' and the prophetic 'word' in terms of the 'stimulus to' and the 'content of' acting as a prophet.[56] The contagious enthusiasm of the *nᵉbī'îm*, by no means disorderly or inarticulate,[57] could overwhelm bystanders (I Sam. 19.20) and rouse in them a similar religious passion. Prophecy was originally a condition, a condition of men driven over the land by an enthusiasm for holy war[58] inspired by the divine 'spirit'. The divine 'word' could join with the 'spirit' as the content of the experiences.

The piecemeal character of our records of early prophecy will continue to make such distinctions a matter of contention and Buber admits that the concepts of 'word' and 'spirit' are not sharply distinguished. Nevertheless, his association of the spirit primarily with the physical aspects of ecstasy is important. Lindblom, while commending Buber's analysis, has written of the spirit evoking 'the revelatory state of mind, while the "word" referred to the revelation itself'.[59] This, however, lacks something of Buber's emphasis on the physical manifestations of enthusiasm, which indicated the spirit's activity. And another valuable aspect of Buber's study is his setting together of the word and spirit as complementary rather than as contrasted concepts in the total event of prophecy.

(ii) *The spirit and false prophecy*
If the 'spirit' had played such a large part in 'false prophecy' as Mowinckel suggests,[47] we would expect to find material clearly reflecting this. In fact, he misrepresents the passages on which his argument is based.

To refer once more to I Kings 22: Micaiah does not charge the four hundred prophets with falsehood. It was Yahweh's intention to mislead Ahab, so that the four hundred were *true* rather than *false* prophets, even if they did not fully understand the divine purpose. The passage cannot be taken to imply that those who appealed to the spirit declared only their personal fancies (cf. Jer. 14.14 et al.), or that the spirit regularly misled them. Micaiah affirmed the spirit's message, until he was asked to confirm his prophecy.

Hosea 9.7 reads: 'The prophet is a fool, the man of the spirit is mad.' Mowinckel interprets this to mean that Hosea thought the spirit-inspired man was a 'fool without morality' and so disclaimed all his practices. But far from representing Hosea's own view of the spirit-inspired, this verse quotes the derisive opinion of the prophets commonly held by the people (cf. II Kings 9.11; Jer. 29.26).[60] Notwithstanding his criticism of some prophets (4.5), Hosea held prophecy in high regard. The 'men of the spirit' were no fools or madmen but the watchmen of God's people (9.8; cf. 12.10–13). Amos had also regarded the *nebī'īm* as Yahweh's gift to Israel (2.11).

Micah 3.8: 'I am filled with power, with the spirit of Yahweh' is emended by Mowinckel, who deletes as a gloss all reference to 'the spirit of Yahweh'. But there are no generally accepted grounds for such an emendation.[61] Micah 2.11 may contain some irony in its play on the word *rūaḥ*. Men who purport to instruct the people but do so falsely utter not the counsel of the divine spirit (*rūaḥ*) but mere wind (*rūaḥ*). As for Micah, he was indeed filled with Yahweh's spirit (3.8)!

A similar slight may have been intended when Jeremiah spoke of the prophets becoming 'wind' (*rūaḥ*) in 5.13. Yet Jeremiah was himself regarded as a 'madman' (29.26) and this expression recalls the equation of 'madmen' and 'men of the spirit' in Hos. 9.7. That is to say, Jeremiah may also have been regarded as a 'man of the spirit'.

In one of the much less ambiguous denunciations of 'false prophets' which are found in Jeremiah the challenge is phrased: 'if the *word* of Yahweh is with them (let them intercede with Yahweh of hosts . . .)' (27.18). The prophets have prophesied by Baal (2.8; cf. Deut. 13.1ff.), they have prophesied falsely (5.31), they have run to the people of their own accord without Yahweh

having spoken to them (23.21; cf. Deut. 18.20), they have proclaimed a peace against which Yahweh has set his face in judgment
(28.9). None of these charges contrasts one manner of revelation
with another, the activity of the 'spirit' with the communication of
the 'word'.

Thus the quite evident division within Israel's prophetic ranks
during the period of classical prophecy does not permit the so-
called 'false prophets' to be classed as claimants to 'the spirit of
Yahweh'. There is, on the contrary, some evidence that the concept continued to play a part in prophecy. But while there are no
grounds for asserting that there was conscious avoidance of a mis-
used concept,[62] the idea of 'the spirit' seems to have been neglected, or perhaps taken for granted, in pre-exilic classical prophecy. It did not convey the same sense of intimacy with the
divine will as did the 'word'. And being associated more with
features of physical vitality and ecstasy which had lost their early
significance, the activity of 'the spirit' was inappropriate to
describe the predominant characteristic of prophetic experience.
Revival of interest in it awaited a time when physical and ecstatic
factors would again be of importance in the prophets' understanding of the forces enabling them to fulfil their callings.

(iii) *Characteristic concepts of the spirit's activity in Ezekiel and Kings*
We have already considered in some detail the passages I Kings
18.12 and II Kings 2.16. Taken together, they are evidence of the
belief that Elijah could be conveyed physically from place to
place by 'the spirit of Yahweh'. That is one of the 'parapsychic
faculties', the Old Testament examples of which Widengren has
assembled, largely from the reports of prophetic activities in
Kings.[63] Ability to demonstrate extraordinary visual or auditory
powers, the production of food, the neutralizing of poisons,
action from a distance and the bringing about or prediction of
death, were further evidence of a person's freedom from the
physical limitations of ordinary men. Similar activities marked the
new vitality evident in the early Christian community.[64] They
represent a continuous strand of experience 'from the primitive
right up to the most highly evolved religions'.[65] Even today
Papua New Guinean sorcerers are believed to exercise such powers
at will.

In Ezekiel, the verb *nś'*[66] is used of the effect on the prophet of 'spirit' or 'a spirit' (*rūaḥ*) on six occasions.[67] *rūaḥ* lifts the prophet up and 'takes' (*lqḥ*) or 'brings' (*bw*, hiph.) him from the scene of the inaugural vision to the exiles, or from the exile group to Jerusalem and back, or from one part of the temple environs to another. In some cases the experience is directly associated with Ezekiel's awareness of 'the hand of Yahweh' upon him.[68] A number of scholars have felt compelled to dismiss these allusions to translocation. In particular, the claim to having been spiritually transported to Jerusalem was regarded as a literary figure, concealing the fact that for a part of his life Ezekiel prophesied in Palestine.[69] Such a problem of translocation is certainly unique in canonical prophecy. But to suggest the accounts are a literary fiction is to raise a problem of equal magnitude. For no satisfactory explanation has yet been given for the supposed editing of prophecies first delivered in Jerusalem to make it appear that they were delivered in exile.[70] Understood in the context of his own world view, Ezekiel's reports of spiritual removal to Jerusalem are more credible. And if we accept the accounts as genuine attempts to relate prophetic experiences in concepts deriving from pre-classical prophetic tradition, we will find a point of reference for interpreting other aspects of the prophecy.

We have noticed that 'the hand of Yahweh' may be associated with the gift of physical power, as when Elijah 'runs' before Ahab's chariot (p. 16). It may also indicate the occasional alienation of an individual's mind from its normal state, as when Elisha has a musician play as an aid to attaining divine instruction. It appears to be in the second sense that 'the hand' comes upon Ezekiel in association with the activity of *rūaḥ*. Awareness of an extraordinary state of mind may be accompanied by the sense of actual removal from place to place. The activity of 'the hand' and *rūaḥ* in Ezekiel may thus be distinguished and may also, on occasions, be referred to separately.[71] These points of agreement between the prophetic experiences reported in Kings and Ezekiel indicate the close relationship between these prophetic traditions. There are also some differences. But they are due to the refinement of ideas in the later tradition.

In Ezekiel it is generally *rūaḥ* (without the article, and so rendered either 'spirit' or 'a spirit') which conveys the prophet from place to place. In Kings it is *rūaḥ Yahweh* ('a spirit' – or 'the spirit of Yahweh') which is spoken of. Only two passages in

Ezekiel refer specifically to 'the spirit of Yahweh' in relation to prophetic experience (11.5; 37.1), while one speaks of 'the spirit of God' in the same regard (11.24). Moreover, since the phrases in 11.5 and 11.24 are out of character with other parts of the book,[72] 37.1 alone is a firm witness to the prophet's appeal to 'the spirit of Yahweh'. The curious reluctance to use the phrase indicates a facet of Ezekiel's thought which is neglected by those who too readily equate 'spirit' in 2.2; 3.12; etc. with 'the spirit of Yahweh'.[73] The word '*rūaḥ*' is used some fifty times in the book, with a variety of meanings.[74]

Some of the radical conclusions reached by Volz in his study of the spirit of God[75] have long since been called in question. Dürr considered that Mosaic religion was capable of drawing the activities of all demons and spirit-beings under the control of Yahweh at a much earlier period than Volz suggested.[76] Of 'the spirit of Yahweh' which endowed the judges, Eichrodt allows that only the reference in Judg. 3.10 comes from a comparatively late hand.[77] Even the spirit personified in I Kings 22.21–24 was an emissary of Yahweh and under his control. There is, then, no reason to deny that Ezekiel could have known of 'the spirit of Yahweh' as an effective power, both in prophecy and in the leadership of Israel. Yet apart from the throne vision[78] the concept is clearly referred to as 'the spirit of Yahweh' (or 'my spirit' etc. with reference to Yahweh), only in connection with the restoration of the nation, or the revival of the people as those who 'know Yahweh'. Elsewhere 'spirit' or *rūaḥ* may well be understood in terms of 'wind' or 'breath'. The former of these words is widely regarded as the original meaning of *rūaḥ*, but in the Old Testament both wind and breath were thought to derive ultimately from Yahweh. Both were within his power to send forth or withdraw.[79] Thus, when we associate the *rūaḥ* which lifts and transports the prophet with 'wind', it is not to attribute the translocation to some 'natural cause'. It is rather to recognize in the word-play on *rūaḥ*, which is an important feature of the book, the prophet's intention of associating some forces with common physical phenomena. The singular 'spirit of Yahweh', however, is used with respect to a unique event. By reserving this term for prophecies of Israel's revival (see 36.27; 37.14; 39.29; as well as 37.1), the importance of their subject is emphasized. When 'the spirit of Yahweh' is involved in the translocation of Ezekiel in

37.1[80] the verbs *ns'*, *lqh* and *bw'* (hiph.) are missing. Instead *ys'* (hiph., 'bring out') and *nwh* (hiph., 'set down') are used of the spirit's activity and further distinguish the episode from other such experiences. 'The spirit of Yahweh' is thus specifically appealed to here as the instrument of prophetic translocation, in anticipation of perhaps the most significant event of Ezekiel's life, namely, the prophecy of Israel's resuscitation.

The reserve with which 'the spirit of Yahweh' is referred to in Ezekiel does not affect the essential coherence between the traditional representation of translocation in Kings and Ezekiel. Rather it reflects the influence of a different way of thinking on the latter. In the priestly view of the relation between God and the world, natural forces closely reflected divine activity.[81] Thus, the Psalmist looked to the winds as messengers of God (Ps. 104.4). So too, it appears that Ezekiel found an acceptable frame of reference for the understanding of some part of his prophetic experience in the idea of Yahweh's control of wind and breath. But the prophet emphasized very sharply the difference between the old and the new Israel, between the people's past and future obedience to Yahweh. In the context of the hope of restoration, common phenomena no longer served as satisfactory images to describe the new, dynamic power which would enable the people to honour Yahweh's name (cf. 36.22ff.). God himself would participate in the life of the community in a radically new way. In 37.1 the promise of the future is realized in the prophet's own experience. Appeal is made to what might be thought of as a particularly direct medium of divine activity in the restored community – the invasive 'spirit of Yahweh'. There is every reason for accepting the allusions to the divine spirit, which are sometimes regarded as later material in the Ezekiel tradition,[82] as flowing directly from the prophet's own experience and activity. And in these allusions are the seeds of both the post-exilic emphasis on the spirit as a unique representative or manifestation of Yahweh on earth, and the prophetic hope of a general out-pouring of the spirit on Israel (Joel 2.28).

The second feature which distinguishes Ezekiel's reports of the effect of 'the spirit (of Yahweh)' on him from the references in Kings is the mention of 'visions of God' (*mar'ot* *elōhīm*, 8.3; 11.24; cf. 40.2). 'Spirit' (*rūah*) lifts Ezekiel and takes him off 'in visions of

God'. Häussermann[83] has said that the word 'vision' (*mr'h*)[84]
elsewhere indicates the vagueness of such communications. He
refers to the nocturnal settings of the revelations in Genesis 46.2
and I Samuel 3.15 and to the associated words 'dream' (*ḥalōm*) and
'riddle' (*ḥīdā*) in Numbers 12.6, 8. This made *mr'h* a suitable term
to express 'the inadequacy of the image' in Ezekiel's theophany.
However, there is nothing in the Genesis and Samuel passages to
suggest that the visions were unclear to those who experienced
them. And while Numbers 12.6–8 presents problems in its text
and tradition history, it affirms that visions were an accepted
means of prophetic revelation. Johnson relates the use of the
noun *mr'h* to that of the verb *r'h* ('to see') when the latter introduces visions in Isaiah, Amos, Jeremiah, etc. Such visions may of
course involve auditory as well as visual phenomena.[85] This
broader perspective is more appropriate for understanding the
term 'visions of God' in Ezekiel. Zimmerli also suggests that this
expression derived from the old schools of seers.[86] This is
indicated by the use of the word 'Elohim', since in formulations of
his own which involve a divine name Ezekiel uses 'Yahweh'.

   Lindblom, whose concern to clarify the nature of prophetic
experience is well known, refuses to distinguish firmly between the
ways in which 'seers' and 'prophets' received their revelations,
although he suggests broad principles for identifying their
respective activities.[87] But the 'visions' in which seers and prophets
were made aware of future events or distant happenings did not
involve the movement of those who experienced them. In Ezekiel
a new element is introduced. Not only is the degree of the
prophet's participation in the visions themselves – as when he
eats the scroll of woe (3.3) – unparalleled in other Old Testament
vision accounts, but he himself is taken to see visions in distant
places. Some scholars think the words 'in visions of God' in 8.3 and
11.24 were added by followers of the prophet.[88] They, presumably, wished to emphasize the supernatural origin of the experiences.[89] Other scholars think the emphasis on the visionary nature
of the events indicates their essentially visual character. They only
involved seeing distant happenings and the prophet did not feel
himself removed bodily to Jerusalem.[90]

   Widengren, on the other hand, takes such serious account of the
phrase 'in visions of God' as reflecting Ezekiel's own understanding of his experiences, that he distinguishes those accounts

which are and those which are not so qualified. Thus he regards 11.1–13, in which reference is made to *rūaḥ* lifting the prophet up, without mention of 'visions', as an experience in which the prophet believed himself to have been physically transported to Jerusalem. But those passages which refer to journeys 'in visions of God' leave it '*in suspenso* as to whether he only had a vision in which *it seemed to him* as if he were removed there'.[91] *bᵉmar'ot* *ᵉlōhim* thus betrays the prophet's own inability to distinguish the precise character of his experiences. In support of his argument, Widengren appeals to the pseudepigraphic first book of Enoch. In this, physical translocation appears to be distinguished from translocation within visionary experience. With regard to Enoch 39.3: 'in those days a whirlwind carried me off from the earth, and set me down at the end of the heavens', Charles remarks that there is 'a real translation here, like Elijah's'.[92] So too, I Enoch 52.1 offers a further example of physical removal. But I Enoch 14.8 reads:

> And the vision was shown to me thus:
> Behold, in the vision clouds invited me and a mist summoned me,
> and the course of the stars and the lightning sped and hastened me,
> and the winds in the vision caused me to fly and lifted me upward,
> and bore me into heaven.

Comparison of such accounts suggests that certain experiences of removal were felt so strongly that the subject felt he was actually taken bodily to the scene of the events. At other times, and more frequently, such feelings were less intense and were reported as visionary phenomena in which the subject only imagined that he was present at the scene of the vision.[93]

Before discussing further the nature of Ezekiel's experiences of translocation, a third distinction between them and the reports concerning Elijah should be mentioned. In Ezekiel 8.1–3 we find a new divine agent introduced. One having the likeness of a man[94] stretches out his hand and takes (*lqḥ*) the prophet by a lock of his hair.[95] It is together with this figure that *rūaḥ* lifts the prophet up 'between earth and heaven'. This expression, comments Widengren, clearly indicates that Ezekiel experienced the phenomenon of levitation.[96] The appeal to the second agent, as well as the reference to a part of the prophet's person, seems to emphasise that Ezekiel's whole being was involved in the dramatic event. Yet it is this instance of translocation that is specifically said to be a visionary experience.

Some of the events related in the course of Ezekiel's experiences 'in Jerusalem' could be construed as actual happenings. Such events would confirm the view of those who believe Ezekiel prophesied for a time in Palestine.[97] Thus there is some evidence in Jeremiah and Kings that Josiah's reformation was short-lived.[98] But while this may rightly indicate a decline in reforming zeal and the increasing influence of foreign practices after Josiah's death, we cannot on that evidence verify the highly stylized account of the temple worship in Ezek. 8.[99] In any case, the six officers and the man clothed in linen (ch. 9), the bones which come together at the prophet's command (ch. 37), and the details of the new temple (chs 40ff.), can hardly be regarded as anything other than mental images. So too were the visions of other prophets,[100] even though to them the visions were also potent symbols of imminent realities. Why then were the visual images of Ezekiel not simply reported in the more usual pre-exilic style of vision account,[101] such as 'I saw'[102] or 'Yahweh showed me'?[103] Such forms are clearly in evidence in the accounts of pre-classical prophecy.[104] These common forms are also found in considerable number in Ezekiel,[105] but it seems they must have been inappropriate to express at least some of the prophet's experiences.

Zimmerli has stressed rather too strongly the inaccessibility of biographical material concerning Ezekiel.[106] It was certainly not the main intention of Ezekiel or his followers to record details of his personal life, and Howie has rightly rejected the attempt of Broome[107] to psychoanalyse, in terms of Freudian concepts, an individual so far removed from us in time and social background.[108] Yet Ezekiel's life was regarded as a prophetic sign to his contemporaries.[109] Such details as do emerge must be understood, as far as possible, in the context of Ezekiel's own environment and conceptual sphere. And within this, if we admit the influence of certain pre-classical prophetic traditions, there existed some appreciation of the phenomenon of translocation or levitation.

The evidence of physical levitation in controlled circumstances is admitted, even by scholars sympathetic toward psychical research, to be exceedingly slight.[110] No conclusive proof is available to support the many accounts of saints and mediums 'flying in the air' and voyaging to distant places, including heaven and hell.[111] But account must be taken of the fact that such reports do exist and that they have been thought to involve the subjects physically. Some material is to be found in the works referred to in footnotes above. More recent accounts are to be found in the publications of such groups as the Society for Psychical Research.[112] There is no doubt at all in the minds of many Melanesians that sorcerers are readily able to 'fly' from one place to another, although few accounts of observations are recorded.[113]

It is not possible to establish the degree to which suggestibility and hypnotism have influenced those who claim to have experienced or observed such events. But there is evidence of what might be termed the 'real subjective awareness' of translocation or levitation. The indications are that even the simple expedient of breath control may be employed, as in Yoga, to produce feelings of abstraction, insight and levitation.[114] That these are reports of genuine conscious states and not merely fictitious imaginings, is confirmed by the investigations of W. Penfield, of the Montreal Neurological Institute. In the course of neuro-surgical operations, Penfield has identified a region of the brain, by the stimulation of which he has been able to induce a variety of abnormal states of mind in his patients.[115] Hallucinations of a visual or auditory kind, or both, may be reported, and frequently the subjects feel themselves to be in another place.[116] Such feelings are similar to those experienced by patients during seizures before they were operated on. And the hallucinations have in them, according to Penfield, some reproduction of remembered experience, not as single pictures or sounds, but as progressive, changing awareness.[117]

Feelings of levitation are nowadays likely to be described as 'dream-like' states, or considered as moments of alienation between the conscious self and one's body.[118] But former generations may not have been able to make so precise an analysis.[119] II Corinthians 12.1–4 is the most refined account of translocation and visionary experience in the biblical traditions. Yet Paul could not discern the exact nature of his involvement in his heavenly 'visions and revelations of the Lord'.[120] 'Whether (they were) in the body or out of the body I do not know – God knows' (II Cor. 12.2).

Widengren is right, therefore, to have emphasized the ambiguity of many reports of visionary experiences and he has made an important contribution to the understanding of Ezekiel's mysterious journeys. But it is questionable whether he should have isolated 11.1–13 as a unique experience of levitation and one in which, on account of the 'perfect coherence of the logic of the events'[121] and the intensity of the experience,[122] the prophet firmly considered himself to have been bodily involved. If Ezek. 11.1–13 is to be treated as an instance of certain awareness of physical translocation, so too must 37.1–14, for this passage is not said to be a visionary experience either. Also, we have seen that 8.1–10.22; 11.22–25,[123] the passage twice described as a visionary event, is that which most clearly portrays the prophet's sensation of bodily removal. These too should be taken as evidence that Ezekiel was aware of sensations of levitation, potential for which appears to be a constant factor in human experience.

It remains difficult to ascertain the extent to which 'the components of auto-suggestion . . . and the exaggerating influence of later legend'[124] have played a part in the prophet's experiences and in the recording of them. Certainly it is possible that once the experience of translocation was described it became a literary figure used more widely in the course of the book's transmission. For example, this is likely to have been the origin of the present, extended, literary vision-account of chs 40–48.[125] But it is difficult to believe that the references to translocation were without foundation in Ezekiel's own experience, particularly if Ezekiel is to be regarded as in some measure the author of the written prophecy.[126] Dürr, in his investigation of Ezekiel's influence on apocalyptic tradition, does not regard the translocations as literary figures of the kind found in apocalypses, although he considers them to be 'purely spiritual journeys'.[127] Nor does Buttenwieser, who also examines the relationship between Ezekiel and apocalyptic literature, deny the reality, for the prophet, of the visionary voyages. On the contrary, 'these, it must be emphasized, are by no means a mere literary device'.[128]

To summarize: there are in the translocation accounts of Ezekiel significant similarities to the conception and description of the spirit's part in the pre-classical prophetic narratives of Kings. A certain refinement of thought appears to distinguish the references to translocation in Ezekiel, however. 'Wind' rather than 'the spirit of Yahweh' is the instrument effecting the prophet's movement, and a heavenly being, distinct from Yahweh himself, is sometimes appealed to as an agent of and guide in such experiences. There is also some awareness of the imaginary character of the translocations, reflected in their description as moments of visual perception. It seems, therefore, that the allusions in Kings to bodily translocation by the activity of 'the spirit of Yahweh' are earlier than Ezekiel. But as a successor to the pre-classical prophetic tradition, Ezekiel's prophecy owes much of its present character to a similar understanding and representation of prophetic experience.

C. *Demonstration of the divine nature in history:*
     'That you may know that I am Yahweh'

There is a phrase frequently repeated in Ezekiel: 'and you shall know that I am Yahweh'. In his study 'Das Wort des göttlichen Selbsterweises',[129] Zimmerli has described a prophetic form of which he believes these words were a part. In Ezekiel the phrase is freely enlarged upon and to determine its formal usage we must look elsewhere.

I Kings 20.13 and 28 report that certain prophets gave Ahab favourable information from Yahweh during the king's struggles with Syria. In both cases the prophetic words consist of three sections, the middle one of which basically involves the simple prediction: 'See, I am giving him into your hand'. Von Rad has identified this as a form of reply to specific questions in the context of holy war.[130] It could be uttered by priests and by judges[131] as well as by prophets.[132] The stereotyped phrase thus goes back to an early stage in the development of prophetic speech forms, back, in fact, to a time when priests and prophets were not clearly distinguished. The form was used when a leader of the people asked Yahweh whether battle should be joined with Israel's enemies. The reason for the answer is given briefly in the first section of the prophecy. This is straightforward in I Kings 20.28: 'Because the Syrians have said, "Yahweh is a god of the hills, not a god of the valleys", . . .'. In I Kings 20.13 a question, 'Have you seen . . .?', takes the place of the causal phrase.[133] In both cases it is implied that Syria, with her great army, scorns the Israelites and their God.

Prophetic declarations of this kind, consisting of two members – the reason for the decision (*die Begründung*) and the oracle itself (*die Ankündigung*)[134] – are by no means uncommon and are even found in the same chapter of I Kings (20.36, 42). Of particular interest, however, is the introduction of a third member, indicating the purpose of Yahweh in fulfilling the prophecies: 'You shall know that I am Yahweh' (*wᵉyādaʿtā* [*wiydaʿtem*] *kî-ʾanî yhwh*). Knowledge in this case would come from an objective sign, namely the defeat of the Syrians.[135] This would show that Yahweh was no 'god of the hills', as the Syrians supposed. By the sign Israel would know Yahweh as he truly was – God, both of the hills and of the valleys.

Although the concise and regularly-ordered structure of the form in I Kings 20.13 and 28 had disintegrated by Ezekiel's period, Zimmerli considers it possible to still trace its influence. In Ezek. 8 the prophet is led about the temple environs and asked 'Do you see . . .?' This corresponds to the motivation clause (*die Begründung*) in I Kings 20.13. The prophecy (*die Ankündigung*) foretelling Yahweh's act of judgment follows in ch. 9. But in this case no mention is made of the purpose of the prophecy – 'that you may know that I am Yahweh'. More frequently in Ezekiel the reason for divine judgment is contained in a causal statement – 'because . . .' as in I Kings 20.28. The purest examples in Ezekiel of the prophetic form are in the prophecies against the nations (chs 25–32), where such causal statements are regularly found.[136] The prophecies of I Kings 20.13 and 28 are also directed against foreign nations, and it is therefore likely that this form originated with prophecies against Israel's enemies.

Fohrer has criticized Zimmerli's study on the grounds that I Kings 20.13f. and 28 'interrupt the context of the narration and are later additions that grew out of the developing tradition'.[137] He believes those prophetic utterances were formulated on the basis of Ezekiel's words by the last Deuteronomic editors of Kings, and there is no justification for asserting that an early prophetic form was taken up and used by Ezekiel several centuries later. But this is not a convincing argument. It is widely recognized that the tradition of Ahab's wars and death in I Kings 20 and 22 derives from a sound historical source.[138] Fohrer himself even considers that the narrator of this material stood sufficiently close to the events for us to attribute to it a ninth-century date of origin.[139]

Wellhausen[140] and others have argued that the prophetic narrative of ch. 20 (vv. 13f., 22, 28, 35ff.) has subsequently been combined with the dynastic record. But the report of prophetic activity coheres well with the account of the strategy of the battle in vv. 13–22,[141] and the support offered Ahab by the nationalistic prophets was appropriate in view of what must have been widespread anti-Aramean feeling in Israel. Also, considerations of style and language do not provide grounds for asserting much later Deuteronomic editorial activity.[142] Von Rad has said of I Kings 20.13f.: 'Here above all is genuine ancient prophecy.'[143] And certainly the vocabulary and concepts composing the prophecies of both v. 13 and the following v. 28 are attested in other early traditions.[144] Thus the weight of evidence is against the view that Ezekiel's words were the basis of those in Kings. But Fohrer's more general criticism of form-historical presuppositions[145] is of relevance here.

Zimmerli has associated Ezekiel with cultic or nationalistic prophets on account of the words 'I am Yahweh' in the third part of the form.[146] For those words signified the presence of Yahweh among his worshippers.[147] The examples in Pss. 50.7 and 81.10: 'Hear, O my people, and I will speak . . . I am Yahweh,[148] your God', suggest that the phrase authenticated words of Yahweh addressed to the assembly. By their announcement God's presence was declared as he spoke through the mouth of the prophet. But there is no question of Ezekiel having had to conform to the normal use of this or any other form of speech, or to the role of the user. It is important to notice that what appears in Kings as a form of prophecy directed against Israel's neighbours appears in Ezekiel also as a prophecy against Israel. This appears most briefly and pointedly in 11.9f. However, in this instance there is no simple, negative answer to the question of Israel's success in conflict with her enemies. The prophecy that Israel will herself be 'given into the hands' of foreigners is explained in terms of Yahweh's judgment upon his people and their being, in consequence, slain by the sword. Moreover, in Ezekiel's prophecies against the nations it is said of non-Israelites that they 'will know that I am Yahweh' (25.5 etc.[136]). Thus not only is the form found in Ezekiel with some parts enlarged upon and, in certain cases, with parts omitted, as we have already noted above, but there has been a radical inversion of its former usage. It is Israel who will

be given into the hands of Yahweh's avengers and Israel's neighbours will acknowledge Yahweh in his historical activity.[149]

Ezekiel's use of elements of speech forms deriving from the
institution of holy war and other aspects of the cult indicates an
important aspect of the prophet's character and intent. And it is an
example of the prophet's own understanding of the divine will
determining the way in which he used traditional speech and
concepts.

D. *The setting of the prophet's face toward the*
subjects of prophecy

On a number of occasions Ezekiel was instructed to 'set his face'
toward people or places as he prophesied.[150] In one instance he
was told to set his face toward a sketch of Jerusalem, as he
modelled the impending siege of the city.[151] The classical prophets
preceding Ezekiel do not refer to such instructions. But in the
narratives concerning Balaam (Num. 22–24) mention is made of
visual contact between an oracle giver and the subject of his words.
And in II Kings 8.11 Elisha is said to have fixed his gaze and
stared at a man who was seeking an oracle from him.

In Num. 24.1 Balaam is said to have 'set his face toward the
wilderness' where Israel was encamped. It was then that the
spirit of God came upon him and he uttered an oracle of blessing
for Israel. Throughout the narrative, however, there is emphasized
the importance of Balaam seeing at least some members of the
people that the Moabite king wished him to curse.[152] Numbers
22–24 combines narratives deriving from both the Yahwist and
the Elohist, although the precise limits of their contributions are
debated. But it appears that the importance of visual contact
between the seer, or diviner, and his subject was understood by the
compilers of both sources. It is also significant that, while the
events concerned are related of a foreign diviner, it is Israel's God
who gives Balaam his visions and the narrative conveys genuine
Israelite conceptions of divination and prophecy.[153]

Fohrer associates the setting of Ezekiel's face toward the subjects of his prophecies with the Balaam narratives and comments
that such acts originally had a magical significance.[154] 'Overlooking' – the act of casting the evil eye – was widely known in the
ancient world as a means of invoking a great variety of malevolent
ends, including the death, illness or loss of property of the victims.

It was thought to be most potent when the subjects were healthy and prosperous. Belief in its effectiveness persists among many societies and attempts to counter it by modern medicine and psychiatry may prove quite fruitless. It is interesting that the means of averting its influence in the ancient world included the wearing of a piece of holy writing, or putting the same at the entrance of one's house.[155]

In II Kings 8.11 the verb 'make to stand' (*'md*, hiph.) is used with 'his face' – (literally 'he made his face stand') – to convey the idea of Elisha gazing fixedly, perhaps in a trance.[156] The verb 'to set' then follows, suggesting the prophet's gaze was concentrated on Hazael,[157] whose future actions are seen by Elisha in his vision. 'Setting one's face' here means perceiving what will happen to the subject of the prophet's gaze by means of second sight. There are no necessarily evil overtones in this.

A third, even less ominous, meaning is implied by 'setting one's face toward' a person or place in the Ugaritic texts of Ras Shamra. In these the phrase is no more than a stylized expression, used either in reporting the delivery of addresses or in referring to the destination of a journey. Messengers of Keret 'set their faces' toward king Pabil and deliver their messages.[158] And a number of times, in the Baal tablets, those about to undertake journeys are said to 'set their faces' toward their destinations.[159]

The instructions to Ezekiel to set his face toward the subjects of his prophecies have more significance than this. Like his acted prophecies (e.g. chs 4 and 12), such gestures were as much a part of Yahweh's message as the words Ezekiel had to speak. Moreover, they are all found in prophecies of doom. And so they have the same ominous meaning as Balaam's overlooking, even though Ezekiel could not actually see many of the people and places he addressed. As with Elisha too, Ezekiel's mind was concentrated on what was shortly to happen to those people and places.

But as well as these points of similarity with pre-classical prophetic conceptions, 'setting one's face' had significance in the sphere of worship and priestly activity. Yahweh is also said to have set his face toward people as a gesture of both divine favour and disfavour. In Ezek. 7.22 it is said that Yahweh will turn away his face so that his people might profane his sanctuary. The implied association between the blessing of Yahweh and the direction of his face toward his people is attested widely and explicitly elsewhere in the Old Testament, most notably in the Aaronic blessing (Num. 6.25f.)[160] But beside the remarkable passage in Ezek. 7 we find references to Yahweh setting his face toward men that they might be cut off from their people, excluded from the sacred community which derived its life from God (14.8). A similar usage is found in the Holiness Code. Yahweh will set his face against the unrighteous (Lev. 17.10; 20.3–6).[161] So, to speak of God – or one of his prophets – setting his face toward people or things was a figurative way of saying that God's own power was active toward them, whether for good or evil. Ezekiel's actions are therefore to be distinguished from magical cursing. For Ezekiel acted at the instruction of Yahweh and as his representative, and not at the request of any man or from personal spite.

E.   *The motif of the prophet sitting in his house*

II Kings 6.32 describes how 'Elisha was sitting in his house and the elders were sitting with him'. In Ezek. 8.1 a similar phrase is found: 'I was sitting in my house and the elders of Judah were sitting before me.' Related passages are found in other narratives concerning these two prophets. They were attended, in their private residences, by the sons of the prophets or by groups of elders, although the purposes of the assemblies are not always stated.[162]

Comments made in S. Herrmann's study of II Samuel 7[163] apparently prompted Zimmerli to suggest the need to clarify the relationship between the above-mentioned prophetic texts and the literary form underlying the Samuel passage.[164] For II Sam. 7.1 begins: 'Now when the king sat in his house . . .'. And such, Herrmann notes, is a typical introduction of an Egyptian literary form termed 'the story of the king' or 'the royal novel'.[165]

Interest in this form was prompted by Jolles' study of ancient sagas earlier this century.[166] Deriving from Egyptian court styles, the form could vary considerably according to circumstances. Often the purpose of the stories was to explain how rites and institutions originated from decisions of the king, or from revelations to him.

There are two main examples of the form in the Old Testament. The first concerns temple building and the Davidic dynasty (II Sam. 7). The second confirms Solomon as David's successor and establishes the theme of Solomon's wisdom (I Kings 3.4–15). But examination of these passages soon reveals how different they are from the prophetic texts of II Kings 6 and Ezek. 8. The commonplace beginning of a 'royal novel' (e.g. 'Now when the king sat in his house . . .') could well be followed by a revelation to the monarch in a dream (I Kings 3.15) or by way of a prophet (II Sam. 7.17). But in the case of the prophetic passages, Elisha (in II Kings 6.32ff.) foretells the coming of the king and his messengers to him as he sits with the elders, and he goes on to predict the end of the prevailing famine. Ezekiel 8.1, for its part, introduces the complex vision of Jerusalem's corruption and its purging at the hands of Yahweh's emissaries. In neither of the prophetic texts is the king the focus of attention. In the former he must himself come to the one 'sitting in his house'. In Ezek. 8–11 the king is not even mentioned. Clearly, if the form of II Kings 6.32ff. and of Ezek. 8.1ff. owes anything to the 'royal novel', the content of the form has altered greatly. The prophet, as Yahweh's spokesman, has displaced the monarch as the central figure in the story. Also, there is nothing to compare with the themes of temple construction or the succession of a wise monarch in either of the prophetic passages. One is a straightforward declaration that plenty will soon overtake dire need. The other is a rejection of the prevailing temple worship and the existing civil authorities. To find why these passages begin with similar situation-motifs we must consider their broader literary characteristics.

In his study of the saga form Jolles distinguished three groups of sagas. The first are family narratives, of which the Old Testament patriarchal stories are examples. The second group deals not with family history, but with narratives concerning the king, his conquests and his struggles. In these, the king stands, as part of a household, like the head of a family, although on a different level. The last group reveals less interest in the time or locality of events, but concerns heroes, whose stories may be introduced by 'long ago,' 'far from here', etc. Of importance, however, is that the events portrayed in this third group are comparable with those which happened to particular families, so that the connection between all three groups is evident. Also, the style and syntax of the three are quite similar.[167]

It is often difficult to distinguish historical narratives from sagas. Bentzen has written that 'historiography in Israel develops from the realm of (saga) and is never completely disengaged from it.'[168] And von Rad has shown how intimately linked with the hero-sagas of the past was the new wide-ranging conception of the historical drama associated with the rise of Israel as a political state.[169] Elements in the style of the saga thus persisted, along with the heightened historical consciousness reflected in the narratives of later periods. They may be found not only in the 'royal novels', in the anecdotal character of the stories affirming the divine choice of the monarch (II Sam. 7; I Kings 3), but also in the prophetic biographies of II Kings 6.32ff. and Ezek. 8ff., when two charismatics foretell Yahweh's miraculous intervention in human affairs and prophecies of death are wonderfully fulfilled. The main ground for associating the prophetic narratives with the form of the 'royal novel' therefore appears to be their common saga style. It is possible that the introduction of the 'royal novel' form to Israel influenced literary styles to a significant degree. But it is un-likely that the situation-motif – ' "So and so" sat in his house' – was exclusively related to the 'stories of the king'.[170]

There was a reason for the choice of that motif to introduce II Samuel 7, however. The 'house' of the king could have particular significance in the context of a 'royal novel', as the play on the Hebrew word for 'house' (*bayith*) throughout the chapter illus-trates. Relating to both a residence and a family group, as well as to a temple, the word *bayith* was appropriate to the subject and contributed to the artistic construction of the story. The choice of the term may be contrasted with those found in other introductory 'sitting' motifs such as those of Gen. 18.1 and 19.1. David sat not at the entrance to his tent as Abraham did, nor at a city gate like Lot, but in 'his house'. And it was 'his house' or dynasty that Yahweh was to ensure the continuation of.

The subject of the narrative was also important in the choice of the situation-motif of the prophetic texts. The participants in II Kings 6.32 and Ezek. 8.1 were together in a house, which, Deuteronomy reminds us, was a place where the traditions of Israel were discussed and reinforced in the minds of the common people (6.7; 11.19).[171] The sitting of the sons of the prophets before Elisha (II Kings 4.38; 6.1) also suggests a scene of instruc-tion,[172] while the sitting together of elders[173] recalls references to the primitive courts of law in which the elders of a community would 'sit' and deliberate at the town gate.[174] But the situation in

II Kings 6 and Ezek. 8 etc. is hardly one of a court of communal judgment. There is no accused 'standing before the judge' (cf. Deut. 19.17). All those present were seated together, just as we read in Judg. 20.26 etc.: 'all the people of Israel . . . sat there before Yahweh.' Indeed 'sitting before' Yahweh appears to have been a technical expression used of people consulting Yahweh, or his priestly or prophetic representatives.[175] That such a situation was in mind is confirmed by the references to the elders inquiring (*drš*) of Yahweh as they sat before Ezekiel (14.3 and 20.1). And in each instance where the situation is described, it is associated with a prophetic word or vision.

The motif of a prophet 'sitting with elders in his house', then, calls to mind a number of Israel's traditional concepts. The general character of the motif is clear, but its use in the 'royal novel' illustrates that it could be closely related to an author's overall purpose. The introductory situation-motif of the prophetic texts appears to have been particularly appropriate in reports of oracular consultations between prophets and community representatives. And there do not appear to be any introductory phrases in pre-exilic canonical prophecy so similar in expression to the situation-statements of II Kings 6.32 and Ezek. 8.1 etc. Thus here there is another link between Ezekiel and his pre-classical prophetic forbears.

F. *The covenant of Yahweh*

A summary of the above features relating Ezekiel's prophecy to the pre-classical prophetic narratives will be given later, when we consider their importance for understanding Ezekiel's prophetic experience and the book of Ezekiel as a whole. But one final matter to which attention should be drawn is the common concern with the covenant between Yahweh and Israel. In I Kings 19.10 and 14 Elijah is said to have made three complaints against his persecutors. They had forsaken Yahweh's covenant, overthrown his altars and slain his prophets with the sword. The order of the accusations is significant. It suggests that the covenant was the principal element of Israelite faith. Priests and prophets might have had responsibilities with regard to the covenant, but it was primary and its upholders had authority only in so far as they were active in fostering knowledge of and obedience to it.

It has been argued that the previous chapter of I Kings, ch. 18, is intended to represent an act of covenant renewal.[176] 'All the people of Israel' were gathered in assembly at Carmel and instructed to choose for or against Yahweh. There is little evidence of exhortation based on Israel's historical traditions (cf. Josh. 24.2–13). But Elijah challenged the people to commit themselves to Yahweh in terms of the situation currently threatening Israel's faith: 'If Yahweh is God follow him; and if Baal is god follow him' (v. 21). Moses, Joshua and Samuel had similarly presented Israel with the choice of following Yahweh or not.[177] It appears in this case to be assumed that what was entailed in following Yahweh was already known by the people. One cannot, at any rate, deny Elijah's part as covenant spokesman or mediator because the covenant precepts are unmentioned. An interesting parallel with the Elohistic tradition of Ex. 24.3–8 is contained in the details of the altar of sacrifice Elijah built or restored. He is said to have taken twelve stones, as symbols of the Israelite tribes, just as the Elohist records that Moses set up twelve pillars around the altar. These points serve to relate Elijah to Moses, Joshua and Samuel in their activities as covenant mediators.

A growing body of opinion holds that prophets came regularly to act as mediators when the covenant between Yahweh and the people was renewed.[178] But it appears to the present author that during the monarchies the kings of Israel and Judah, assisted by priests, normally fulfilled this role, enunciating the conditions of the covenant. The role of the prophets was to support the monarchs with oracles of promise and warning, so that the people might be aware of the implications of their behaviour following assent to the covenant precepts.[179] The reason for Elijah acting as covenant mediator on Mount Carmel is made explicit in I Kings 18.18, where according to the Hebrew text it is said that Ahab and his predecessors, as leaders of the people, had forsaken 'the commandments of Yahweh'. The Septuagint does not refer specifically to 'the commandments', but the equation of obedience to Yahweh with obedience to his commandments may be justified from other parts of the Elijah narratives. For the first commandment of the decalogue, 'You shall have no other gods before me', would seem to be the basis of Elijah's accusation. Further, in ch. 21, the commandments prohibiting murder and covetousness may well have been the grounds of his charge against Ahab in the affair of Naboth's vineyard (v. 19).

Such clear parallels to the decalogue tradition do not occur in accusations elsewhere in the pre-classical prophetic narratives of I Kings 17ff., but we see in Elijah's prophecy against Ahab a foreshadowing of the classical prophets' appeals to divine law in their more extensively elaborated charges.[180] While, as we have already noted, the narratives concerning Elijah should not be regarded as the actual words of the prophet, it is probable that the reasons given for his oracles of judgment were consistent with the emphases of the groups with whom he was associated and by whom the legends concerning him were passed on. Thus, although we must leave detailed consideration of Ezekiel's use of covenant tradition until the next chapter, we may note here another general but nonetheless significant point of similarity between Ezekiel and the northern pre-classical prophets. For the grounding of their prophecies in covenantal tradition allows us to relate Elijah and Ezekiel as zealous protagonists of Yahweh's covenant and the obligations it entailed for Israel.

III

EZEKIEL AND OTHER MAJOR STREAMS OF OLD TESTAMENT TRADITION

Ezekiel had an extremely broad knowledge of his people's religious heritage and he drew on a wide range of prophetic and priestly traditions.[1] Here we must confine ourselves to considering certain parallels with Hosea's prophecy, and to noting the extensive similarities between Ezekiel and Jeremiah, which are important for understanding both the form and content of Ezekiel's work.

Ezekiel has made extensive use of the Sinai/Horeb covenant tradition. Because of this, and in view of the role Levites are likely to have played in transmitting the pre-classical prophetic narratives, we shall also consider briefly the relationship of his work to Deuteronomy and the Holiness Code. For these are practical expositions of the covenant and both may derive from the teaching activity of Levites.

A. *Hosea*

Hosea's allusions to his prophetic heritage have already been mentioned. It has been suggested that they offer evidence of an accumulation of prophetic tradition, at least in northern Israel, which was likely to have been known among both priestly and lay circles of Israelites.[2] Much of the material in Ezekiel which reflects the thought and language of Hosea is also found in other pre-exilic prophecies and in Deuteronomy. Thus evidence of Hosea's direct influence on Ezekiel is slight. Yet the relationship is significant. For it affirms Ezekiel's alliance with the same northern circles as Hosea in their concern to alert Israel to its covenant responsibilities.

A motif which appears to have originated with Hosea is that of Israel, or the land of Israel, as Yahweh's unfaithful wife. Ezekiel makes extensive use of the same theme when he surveys the history of Israel and Judah in chs 16 and 23, although, as is characteristic of Ezekiel, the imagery is greatly elaborated. Isaiah termed Jerusalem a prostitute (1.21) and Jeremiah, as we shall have cause to note again, alludes to Israel and Judah as two faithless sisters (3.6–11). But there are features of the motif in Ezek. 16 which are more directly reminiscent of Hosea's prophecy, according to which Israel is 'decked' (*'ādāh*) with Yahweh's gifts of gold and silver and misuses these – although in different ways – in her cultic activities.[3] Also, it is said that Yahweh himself will uncover the nakedness of the harlot before her lovers.[4]

More important is the fact that, from the same chapter of Ezekiel, it appears the prophet knew a motif of which 'all evidence falls into a relatively narrow sphere of theological history'.[5] This is the so-called *Fundtradition*, according to which Yahweh 'found' Israel in the wilderness and a relationship was established there, as a result of which Israel could be described in such terms of endearment as 'the bride of Yahweh' or 'the apple of his eye'. The theme is alluded to in Deut. 32.10 and Jer. 2.2f.; 31.2f., as well as in Hos. 9.10, and possibly 10.11. Ezekiel relates it to Jerusalem in ch. 16, where the first contact between Yahweh and the personified city takes place when Yahweh comes across an outcast child lying in a field. In vv. 6 and 8 the use of the word 'to see' (*rā'āh*) is paralleled in Hos. 9.10, while the word for 'pass by' (*'ābar*) – which is also thought to have been a technical term within the 'finding' motif[6] – is paralleled in Hos. 10.11.

Another motif recurring in Ezekiel is that of a new exodus. Hosea 2.14 speaks of Yahweh alluring Israel and bringing her into the wilderness (cf. ch. 3; 12.9). Other passages prophesy the return of Ephraim to Egypt (8.13), or to Egypt and Assyria (9.3). It is hardly surprising that such concepts should have had great significance for the prophet Ezekiel, exiled in Babylon. Although we do not learn from Ezekiel of any oppression of the exiles comparable with that suffered by their forbears in Egypt, they certainly felt they had been unjustly treated by their God (18.25; 33.17) and were tempted to cast aside their distinctive faith and adopt the religious customs of their captors (Ezek. 20.32). It was perhaps with such a thought in mind that Ezekiel prophesied a time when Yahweh would once more lead his people from their foreign dwelling and bring them to the promised land (20.33–44). The latter part of Ezek. 20 stands in marked contrast to the preceding historical sketch of the first exodus. The account of Yahweh's first dealings with Israel is full of acts of apostasy. Indeed Ezekiel goes beyond the traditions of rebellion preserved in the so-called 'Book of Israel's Failings'[7] (Num. 11–25; 31). Idolatry was practised by the people even in Egypt (Ezek. 20.8).[8] Hosea and Jeremiah regarded the period of wilderness wandering as in some measure a time of faithfulness to Yahweh,[9] although this should not be taken to indicate that the prophets conceived of a 'nomadic ideal'.[10] As Talmon has argued, the desert continued to be the place of fearful punishment and the desert wandering was only of value in so far as it served to restore the covenant relationship and prepare the people for life in the truly ideal situation, i.e. settled existence in Canaan.[11] So, for Ezekiel, the desert was to be the scene of a great act of judgment in which the rebels would be purged from the people. But the confrontation between Yahweh and Israel, which is described in Hos. 2.14 in terms of endearment – 'I will speak tenderly to her' (lit. 'to her heart') – is portrayed in Ezekel as an awesome encounter – 'face to face' (20.35).

Further points of comparison involve the covenant that will ensure Israel's future security, and the description of what that future holds. The covenant of Hos. 2.18 was one which Yahweh would establish as an independent arbitrator 'for' Israel (*lāhem*[12]), 'with' (*'im*) beasts, birds and reptiles. Ezekiel 34.25–29 develops Hosea's idea, although Yahweh does not now act as a mediator. Israel is one partner to the covenant: 'I will make *for* them a covenant of peace' (*wᵉkāratti lāhem bᵉrīt šālōm*, v. 25). But no second partner is introduced by way of the anticipated preposition *'im* ('with'). Certainly the 'wild beasts' (v. 25) are not the other party to the covenant. They are to be removed from the land.[13] It appears Ezekiel has adapted Hosea's thought to that more commonly found in the Old Testament. The covenant will be made between Yahweh and Israel. The Israelites will again acknowledge that they are Yahweh's people (v. 30). Yet Wolff is right to assert that Ezekiel had his 'model' (*Vorbild*) in Hosea's prophecy.[14] For the promise of peace from the ravages of nature and war, through a covenant that Yahweh will establish 'for'

Israel, is parallel in both content and form to Hosea 2.18. And both prophets emphasize in this way that the future peaceful existence of their people will involve a divine act affecting the whole created order.

There is also envisaged in Hosea 1.11 the reconstitution of Israel and Judah under one 'head or leader' (*rō'š*). This verse has been thought to offer grounds for dating Hosea 1.10–2.1 in the exilic or post-exilic period.[15] It has been regarded as dependent upon Ezek. 37.15ff. (especially vv. 21f.) Wolff, however, has pointed out a number of factors which make it unlikely that the Hosea passage should be attributed to an editor. Its present place in the prophecy interrupts a theme of judgment, and it is introduced by a passive contruction alien to prophetic speech and particularly to oracles of hope elsewhere in Hosea. But these features may simply be due to its interpolation into the once-independent collection of sayings in chs 1–3.[16] As to the late dating which some think necessary to explain the prophecy: there is no mention of the people being gathered from exile among the nations (cf. Ezek. 37.21); the term *rō'š* – as compared with *melek* ('king') in Ezek. 37.22[17] – appears to refer to the Israelite leader prior to the institution of the monarchy (cf. Num. 14.4; Judg. 11.8); while the people's 'rising up from the land' may be understood in terms of Ex. 1.10, where it signifies the seizure or possession of land or property.[18] So the passage was appropriate to the period about 733 BC when Assyria annexed Israelite territory. And as a prophecy that the united people of Israel would conquer the land again, it represents 'a possible first stage'[19] of the prophecy of restoration in Ezek. 37.15ff.

B. *Jeremiah*

The extensive affinities of thought and speech between Ezekiel and his contemporary Jeremiah have been recognized by many commentators and various interpretations of the relationship have been offered. Herntrich regarded it as evidence that Ezekiel was active as a prophet in Jerusalem.[20] Burrows, who advocated the late dating of Ezekiel, believed that the author of the prophecy had the book of Jeremiah before him and regarded it as sacred writing.[21] In his comparative study of the two prophecies, J. W. Miller[22] has suggested that the basis of the relationship was that

Ezekiel had heard Jeremiah prophesying in Jerusalem. He also had access, while in exile, to a copy of Jeremiah's 'prose-words'. Although the picture it presents of the Jeremiah tradition may be 'over-simplified',[23] this thesis is of considerable interest. For it suggests explanations of some important features of the book of Ezekiel.

To consider first the question of the prophets' use of prose: it is extremely difficult to understand how the supposed 'redactors' of Jeremiah and Ezekiel could have been so insensitive and artless as to interpolate great portions of prose writing into these prophetic books, if poetry continued to be a fundamental characteristic of prophetic records in the late seventh and early sixth centuries BC. Fohrer's attempt to reassert the presence of poetry as a criterion of the genuine material in Ezekiel is not successful,[24] and some explanation of the extensive use of prose is necessary.

Both T. H. Robinson and Eissfeldt earlier suggested that Baruch's scroll (Jer. 36.4, 32) originally consisted of the sermon-like prose passages in Jeremiah.[25] Following this idea Miller asserts that the words of the scroll were likely to have been of a simple rhetorical style, so that they would catch the attention of worshippers on the day of festival (Jer. 36.6) and be immediately comprehensible to them.[26] Also, he thinks that the prose material in Jeremiah, scattered though it is, corresponds to the form and content of the covenant renewal preaching, such as we find in Deuteronomy and elsewhere. An historical survey of Yahweh's dealings with Israel[27] is followed by a declaration of covenant law.[28] Curses are pronounced against all who fail to keep the law[29] and the impending misfortunes of such transgressors are illustrated;[30] finally there is a summary of Jeremiah's prophetic activity and the implications of his message.[31] Yet it should be stressed that, for the most part, Jeremiah's words stand in marked contrast to Deuteronomy's. The latter are optimistic – the covenant is capable of fulfilment and its promises and blessings are attainable. With the exception of what may be thought of as the covenant conditions (7.5–7), Jeremiah's covenant preaching contains no promises of blessing but emphasizes that the covenant has been broken on Israel's part and punishment is imminent.

It would be quite incorrect to speak of Jeremiah parodying the Deuteronomic covenant. Rather, he affirms its validity and says it will issue in punishment, 'unless men turn from their evil ways' (Jer. 36.7). In Baruch's scroll – if it is allowed that it was constructed on the pattern of the covenant renewal preaching – we have an example of the use of a cultic form by one who was, at the time, excluded from the cult (Jer. 36.5) and who opposed some aspects of it.[32] Certainly, in the temple sermon (7.2–15) parallels with covenant speech are evident.[33] So it appears we have, in Jeremiah, a prophet who virtually fulfilled the role of a covenant spokesman, although he recognized the monarch's right, or rather, duty, to undertake that role in normal circumstances.[34] This explains both Jeremiah's acquiescence in Josiah's renewal of the covenant,[35] and his prophecy concerning the future ruler: 'I will make him draw near, and he shall approach me, . . . says the Lord' (30.21).[36] But what has often been thought of as characteristic of prophecy – the foretelling of events – is seen now to be subservient to the primary prophetic task, namely helping to maintain the covenant relationship with Yahweh. For the oracles included in Baruch's scroll were intended to awaken men to the implications of that relationship. It should also be noted that, although Jeremiah appears to have used the traditional form of covenant preaching, his prophecies derived from his deep personal encounters with Yahweh. Thus, observing the similarity between one of the oracles in Jer. 16 and the fate of the 'cursed' described in Deut. 28,[37] Miller rightly comments: 'these well-known expressions, in association with the strong personal character of the prophetic message, take on a new intensity'.[38]

We will consider later in this chapter the way in which Ezekiel represents the curses of another stream of covenant tradition in vivid allegories and acted prophecies.

As to the particulars of the various prose passages of Jeremiah: it is possible to identify in them a pattern which is also found in Ezekiel.[39] Mention is made of the word of Yahweh having come to the prophet by the use of the formula: 'and the word of Yahweh came to me (saying) . . .', or some variation thereof.[40] This introduction is followed by a command or other communication. Sometimes mention is made of the prophet's execution of the command.[41] Finally, the public declaration of the meaning of the action or message is introduced with the words: 'thus said Yahweh'. This last and usually longest section is an integral part of the prophetic narrative and not, as Mowinckel has asserted,[42] a secondary appendage. The intention appears to have been to make the message of Yahweh clear and forceful for those who did not know the circumstances in which it was originally delivered.[43]

Jeremiah was active some twenty-nine years before the exile which involved Ezekiel's removal to Babylonia.[44] The scroll which was read in the temple precincts was written approximately six years before the exile.[45] To the material composing the original scroll, destroyed by Jehoiakim (Jer. 36.23ff.), we are told Baruch added 'many words like them' (Jer. 36.32). Miller identifies the additions as 24.1–10; 27 and 35 (which are of similar auto-biographical style), and 21.1–10; 32.1–17a, 24–29a, 42–44 and 34.8–22 (which begin with a considerable amount of introductory material, again suggesting that they were intended for people who did not know the original contexts of the words). Some of the events concerned took place before 598 BC, others about the time of the exile, while some relate to the reign of Zedekiah. However, it is clear from Jer. 29 that the exiles were in contact with Jerusalem, so that later material, including parts of the so-called 'Booklet of Consolation' (Jer. 30–31),[46] could also have been communicated to them.

The reason for distinguishing the above passages of Jeremiah from the remainder of his prophecy is that they especially appear to have influenced the form and content of Ezekiel's work. So far as may be judged, Jeremiah made far more extensive use of auto-biographical prose to communicate and preserve a record of his prophecies than any of his predecessors. Autobiographical prose predominates in the book of Ezekiel. Also, the prose style of both Jeremiah and Ezekiel is characterized by the frequent repetition of words and phrases which the authors appear to have regarded as central to their themes.[47] Catchwords or word-plays are employed for emphasis, as are syntactical variations, in which the object is placed at the beginning of a sentence, or a *hēmmā* ('they') is put at the end, referring back to the subject.[48]

Beside these features of common prose style, words and concepts which are found in the above passages of Jeremiah recur in Ezekiel when the latter is dealing with similar topics. Thus Jeremiah's call, which broadly follows the traditional representation found also in Isaiah,[49] is distinguished from the latter by the establishment of the prophet as a 'fortified city, etc.' against the people. The passage in question begins: 'And I, behold, I have made you . . .' (*wā'ᵃnī hinnē nᵉtattīkā"*, Jer. 1.18). Ezekiel was also able to withstand the rebuffs of his people because Yahweh gave him (*hinnē nāttatī"*) a hard face and forehead (3.8). Jeremiah's words against the lying prophets, who 'are prophesying a false vision and worthless divination and deceit of their hearts' (*ḥᵃzōn šeqer wᵉqesem [we]ᵉlil wᵉtarmīt libbām hēmmā mitnabbᵉᵉîm*, 14.14), are recalled by Ezekiel's sayings about 'a false vision and flattering divination' (*ḥᵃzōn šāwᵉᵉ ūmiqsam ḥālāq*, 12.24) and concerning those who 'prophesy out of their hearts' (*hammitnabbᵉᵉōt millibbᵉhen*, 13.17).[50] Also, when Ezekiel's wife dies he is commanded 'Do not mourn nor weep' (*lōᵉ tispōd wᵉlōᵉ tibke*, 24.16). This is distinctly reminiscent of the instruction in Jeremiah: 'Do not go to mourn and do not lament for them' (*ᵉal-tēlēk lispōd wᵉᵉal-tānōd lāhem*, 16.5), and both passages anticipate the imminent destruction of Jerusalem.

On occasions Ezekiel has taken up Jeremiah's ideas and elaborated them at length, sometimes by combining them with other prophetic and even extra-biblical material. We have already noted Ezekiel's use of Hosea's concept of Israel as Yahweh's wife. Jeremiah developed the motif to embrace the concept of Israel and Judah as 'sisters' (3.6–11).[51] Two features which appear first in Jeremiah and then in Ezekiel are that Jerusalem/Judah 'saw' (*tēreᵉ*) the sins of the faithless Israel and her misdeeds became even greater. In Ezekiel reference is made to a third wicked sister, Sodom (16.44–58). In comparison with Jerusalem, her two sisters appeared righteous (16.51). But these verses are a later expansion and not part of the primary tradition. So the concept of comparative guilt is better illustrated in 23.1–27, where again there is emphasis upon the example of the elder sister, Samaria, which Jerusalem 'saw' (*tēreᵉ*, v. 11).

Oesterley and Robinson have described Ezek. 23 as a 'sermon' on the text of Jer. 3.6–11.[52] This is a pertinent comment on the direction of influence. Ezekiel appears to be the borrower, here and elsewhere, of Jeremiah's language and thought.[53] Again, Ezek. 36.24–28 recalls Jeremiah's prophecy of the new covenant (31.31–34) so clearly that von Rad has said 'one feels that Ezekiel must somehow have had Jeremiah's prophecies in front of him'.[54] Yet Ezekiel also moulds what he borrows very much according to his own convictions. Thus the 'bones' which Jeremiah sees strewn on open ground (8.1–3) are the 'bones' whose flesh and spirit are restored, that they might live again (Ezek. 37.1ff.). Or when Ezekiel is asked, 'Do you see . . .?' what perversions are being committed[55] in place of the true worship of Yahweh, he goes far beyond Jer. 7.16–20 in his carefully stylized description of acts of apostasy performed in every part of the temple precincts (Ezek. 8). And Ezekiel's references to the gift of a new heart and spirit (11.19; 36.26), rather than of Yahweh putting his law within men and writing it on their hearts (Jer. 31.31ff.), suggests he saw the need of a more radical renewal of the nation's life.

The parallels between Ezekiel and the remaining material in Jeremiah – the poetic oracles and the biographical excerpts – are by no means negligible.[56] But Miller, and Fohrer also,[57] have drawn attention to the occurrence elsewhere in the Old Testament of words, phrases and motifs which are sometimes thought to relate Ezekiel to Jeremiah. Many appear to have been used widely in Ezekiel's period or are found in such different contexts in the two prophecies that there are inadequate grounds for asserting Ezekiel's literary dependence. The parallels are, however, numerous enough to suggest to Miller that Ezekiel had heard Jeremiah prophesying in Jerusalem, or at least that he had some knowledge of his prophecies other than those included in Baruch's scroll and the associated material, a written copy of which he either possessed or had access to while in exile. Earlier Robinson suggested that 'Ezekiel had heard Jeremiah in the days before the captivity of Jehoiachin'.[58] And Skinner had written: 'We may safely assume that amongst the treasures which [Ezekiel] took with him into exile was the roll written by Baruch to the dictation of Jeremiah in the fourth year of Jehoiakim (Jer. 36)'.[59]

We cannot verify the fact that the exiles took documents such as Baruch's scroll with them to Babylon, or that a copy of the scroll was available to them there. As Bright puts it, the scroll was in a 'limited edition'.[60] There is evidence that Ezekiel knew a tradition of written prophecy, for in the account of his call he was given a scroll to eat which was covered with prophecies of doom (2.8–3.3). But the thought of Ezekiel delivering or recording his prophecies with one eye on a copy of Baruch's scroll is incongruous. The scroll was, however, Jeremiah's own testimony to the faithful fulfilment of his calling. So it was likely to have been the focus of attention among those who recognized the truth of his words and tried to reinforce them. It has been shown that oral transmission was an important means, beside the written word, of accurate communication in the ancient world, and the transmission of such material as the scroll by word of mouth is sufficient to account for the parallels noted above. For there is no evidence of slavish quotation and the characteristics of the prose style that have been pointed out were not typical of Jeremiah and Ezekiel alone.[61] Thus while it cannot be denied that Ezekiel could have read Baruch's scroll, or that he could have heard Jeremiah in person, his knowledge of Jeremiah's words may simply derive from oral tradition in both Judah and Babylon.

C. *Deuteronomy*

Sometimes distinctions between Ezekiel and the Deuteronomic tradition have been stressed in order to show how much more closely the prophet was allied with the authors of the Priestly writings (P) and the Holiness Code (H).[62] On the other hand, the points of agreement between Ezekiel and Deuteronomy (D) have sometimes been emphasized, in order to prove the prophet's knowledge of and sympathy with many of the Deuteronomic concerns. Those who have adopted the latter viewpoint[63] do not deny that in many instances Ezekiel reflects more clearly the vocabulary and concepts of P and H. But they do rightly argue that the prophecy as we have it presupposes the existence of Deuteronomy.

As in the case of Hosea, there is relatively little evidence of Deuteronomy's direct influence on Ezekiel. The main reason for this is that Deuteronomy is paralleled in many respects by the Holiness Code.[64] Welch explained the similarities on the analogy of the Elohistic and Yahwistic narratives. Just as these represent the northern and southern versions of the common traditions of Israel, so D and H represent the northern and southern versions of the laws deriving ultimately from the Book of the Covenant.[65] Although opinion is divided on the actual place of origin of H, a number of scholars associate it with Jerusalem.[66] And it would have been natural for Ezekiel to draw on a tradition from his own area whenever it was parallel to Deuteronomy.

Both Ezekiel and Deuteronomy, as well as the Holiness Code, regarded Yahweh's statutes and judgments as standards by which all aspects of Israelite life were to be regulated.

In Ezek. 18.5–9 the preconditions of righteousness are set out in the form of a priestly 'entrance liturgy'. Most of the prohibitions and commands have close parallels in the Holiness Code or in the Book of the Covenant, but one (Ezek. 18.6) appears to reflect the distinctive emphasis of Deut. 12.1ff. So it is forbidden 'to eat upon the mountains', i.e. to partake of sacrificial meals at local sanctuaries. The implication of this verse – that the cults of the local sanctuaries were profane – is made explicit elsewhere.[67] It is true that Ezekiel includes Jerusalem in his condemnations of idolatrous sanctuaries (ch. 8). But this is hardly reason to assert that Ezekiel was concerned only with the perversion of the cult and not with its centralization.[68] For in his vision of the restored community a single sanctuary is described (40.1–42.20), which was to serve as a cultic centre for all the people. Since it is possible that the tradition common to the prophet and the Holiness Code did not demand a centralized cult,[69] the influence of the Deuteronomic reform movement may be discerned here.

The idolatry of Israel is allegorized in terms of harlotry in Ezek. 16 and 23. The punishment prophesied is death by stoning and by the sword.[70] Punishment by stoning is also prescribed for adulteresses in Deut. 22.21. But the main reason for Ezekiel's accusation against the harlots was their participation in foreign cults. So it may be that the idea of stoning the accused was also suggested by Deut. 13.10, where stoning is prescribed for those who lead their kindred to serve other gods.[71]

Among the phrases which have been held to affirm Ezekiel's literary dependence on Deuteronomy is 'with a strong hand and an outstretched arm' (Ezek. 20.33f.). This phrase, as we have already observed, is characteristic of Deuteronomy and in both the prophecy and the law code it is used with reference to an exodus experience. The concept of Yahweh as the inheritance of the Levites (Ezek. 44.28) is another characteristic of Deuteronomy, though also of P.[72] That the priests should be permitted 'to stand before Yahweh to minister to him' suggests to Burrows[73] that an expression typical of Deuteronomy[74] has been used in Ezek. 44.15. However, he admits that the phrase is likely to have had wide currency in priestly circles.

Haag acknowledges the linguistic parallels between the description of the fruitful land in Ezek. 36.29f. and the Deuteronomic tradition.[75] The word 'corn' (*dāgān*) appears frequently in Deuteronomy – including Deut. 7.13 – but not in the Holiness Code and only here in Ezekiel. 'Famine' (*rā'āb*) is threatened in Deut. 28.48, but nowhere in H or P, while the word 'increase' or 'produce' (*tᵉnūbā*) is found in the Pentateuch only in Deut. 32.13. But it is also significant, as Haag emphasizes, that although the land is to be made fruitful in response to Israel's obedience, Deuteronomy attributes Yahweh's concern for Israel to his love (7.12f.), while Ezekiel attributes it to concern for the honour of his name (36.22ff.) The words 'love' (*'āhēb*) and 'kindness' (*ḥesed*) are never found in Ezekiel with Yahweh as their subject. Yet lest this fact should be taken to indicate the harshness of Ezekiel's conception of Yahweh, it should be remembered that he is portrayed as a God who showed compassion to a repulsive outcast and lavished his attentions on an undeserving Israel. The Deuteronomists too stressed Israel's unworthiness as an object of Yahweh's concern (Deut. 7.6ff. etc.), and it seems to have been Ezekiel's intention to emphasize the magnitude of this divine grace. Also, when the prophet speaks of Yahweh acting 'for the sake of his name' he was alluding not to divine self-interest, but to the necessity of Yahweh vindicating his character as a God of compassion and forgiveness, as well as of uncompromising wrath against the impenitent (cf. Deut. 7.10 etc.). While Yahweh's nature as a just God demanded Israel's destruction, his compassionate nature also made possible Israel's restoration. For he desired not the death of the wicked, but their repentance, in order that they might 'live' (Ezek. 18.23, 32; 33.11).[76]

Both Fohrer and S. Herrmann[77] have commented on the similarities between Ezekiel's word of promise for the exiles in 11.14–21 and various passages in Deuteronomy. Thus the prophet is said to have taken up the threat of exile in Deut. 4.25ff. (cf. especially Ezek. 11.16 and Deut. 4.27). He prophesies their eventual gathering and restoration (cf. Ezek. 11.17 and Deut. 30.3–5), and he anticipates their obedience to Yahweh's statutes, so that they might live as his people (cf. Ezek. 11.20 and Deut. 7.6; 26.16–19). Fohrer is careful to preface his remarks by suggesting that Ezekiel was reflecting the theology of his period and affirms the prophet's independent use and modification of the Deuteronomic material. Reventlow, on the other hand, has attempted to show that the tradition Ezekiel shares with the Holiness Code is the basis of the prophecy.[78] It is true that the catchwords 'countries' (*'ᵃrāṣōt*) and 'nations' (*gōyim*) appear in Ezek. 11.16, in contrast to Deuteronomy's 'people's' (*'ammīm*,

4.27). And the formulation of the phrase: 'they will walk in my statutes and keep my judgments and obey them' (Ezek. 11.20), is closer to Lev. 26.3 than to Deut. 26.16. But it is not satisfactory to associate Ezek. 11.19 with the Holiness Code and ignore its similarity to Deuteronomy. For a point of considerable importance is Ezekiel's reference to the 'new heart'[79] which Yahweh will give to the exiles. The heart is obliquely referred to once in the Holiness Code as the medium of human response to the divine will (Lev. 26.41), but it is frequently referred to in such a way in Deuteronomy (6.5 etc.). This characteristic conception of the Deuteronomic tradition helps explain the divergence between Jeremiah's prophecy of the new covenant and the parallel prophecies in Ezekiel,[80] in which the gift of a new heart makes possible the observance of Yahweh's statutes and judgments (Ezek. 11.20; 36.27; cf. Deut. 26.16).

Ezekiel's attitude to the priesthood has frequently been thought to offer grounds for dating his activity after the appearance of Deuteronomy. The prophecy distinguishes between priests and Levites on account of the Levites' misguidance of the people, and it thereby stands in contrast to Deuteronomy's liberal attitude toward Levites in general. So radical a rebuff to one of Deuteronomy's major concerns may even be thought to call in question the prophet's sympathy with the law code as a whole. Admittedly, those who discount completely the prophet's part in formulating the closing chapters of Ezekiel may ignore the distinction. But if the vision of the new Jerusalem in Ezek. 40–48 is in any respect to be attributed to the prophet, some consideration of the divergence from Deuteronomy is necessary.

It must be borne in mind that, while Deuteronomy recognized that all Levites were not active as priests, it did imply that all priests were Levites.[81] The latter point appears to have been emphasized by what Gese, in his study of Ezek. 40–48,[82] has termed 'the redactor'. For the words 'the priests, the Levites' (*hakkōhᵃnīm halᵉwiyyīm*) are found in Ezek. 43.19, among ritual directions in which the priests are referred to simply as 'the priests' (43.24, 27). A further stage in the development of the tradition can also be discerned. Ezekiel 40.45–46a also makes no mention of distinctions between priests in terms of lineage. Only in what may be regarded as a secondary appendage – 'they are the sons of Zadok' (v. 46b) – are the Zadokites (as a sub-group of the Levites) specifically mentioned. And with this passage may be compared the words: 'who are of the seed of Zadok' in 43.19. Gese attributes both phrases to a 'glossator', associating them with the 'Zadokite stratum' which is most clearly in evidence in Ezek. 44.6ff. There it is said that the Levites will become 'keepers of the charge of the temple' (*mišmeret habbāyit*, 44.14) in contrast to the Zadokites who will remain 'keepers of the charge of the sanctuary' (*mišmeret miqdāš*, 44.15).[83] This distinction in terminology is also reflected in 45.4f. and 46.24. But in the second passage concerning the apportionment of land (ch. 48, cf. ch. 45), although a distinction between 'priests' and 'Levites' is presupposed in the primary narrative it is only in v. 11 that the priests are identified as Zadokites. That the verse is an interpolation is suggested by the use of the first person singular suffix with *mišmeret* – reading 'my charge' – in a passage in which the subject, Yahweh, is spoken of in the third person. From these considerations, it appears that the original instructions regarding the priesthood were first revised in order to specify that all priests were Levites. As a result of later revision priests and Levites were distinguished. Finally the difference in function of the two groups was established and the priests were identified as Zadokites.

It is difficult to conceive of Ezekiel himself having excluded the Zadokite priesthood from responsibility for the corrupt state of the Israelite cult. Jerusalem was worse than Samaria in the depths of iniquity to which she had sunk and in his portrayal of worship at the temple (ch. 8) it is likely that an allusion to the priesthood was intended. For Ezek. 8.16–18 represents the climax of the scenes of apostasy. The corrupt worship of the elders and women of Israel had already been observed, and the last scene takes place immediately in front of the temple. The only objection to supposing that an allusion to the priests was intended is the words 'the elders' in Ezek. 9.6. The executioners of punishment were to begin with 'the elders' in front of the temple. But the words are rightly treated as an explanatory gloss by many scholars,[84] and it is apparent that the men at the entrance of the temple are contrasted rather than equated with the elders of Ezek. 8.11.

Like Jeremiah, Ezekiel at first took a much more pessimistic view of his nation's future than Deuteronomy. He was to announce the

punishment from Yahweh for Israel's neglect of the covenant. But
it should be evident from the above that Ezekiel was not in conflict with Deuteronomy. There are some significant similarities
between the two. And Ezekiel certainly agreed with Deuteronomy's emphasis on the need for reform of his people's moral and
cultic behaviour.

D. *The Holiness Code*

There are many parallels, both of vocabulary and modes of expression, between Ezekiel and the Holiness Code.[85] But despite their
number, the parallels are too brief to show clearly the direction of
literary influence. Thus virtually every possibility of relating the
prophecy and the law code has been advocated by one scholar or
another in the course of the last century. Some have regarded the
law code as older and as a literary source on which Ezekiel was
dependent.[86] Others have maintained the priority of Ezekiel and
considered either the prophet himself or one of his disciples to
have been the author or redactor of the Holiness Code.[87] Division
of the law code into various strata has even enabled some parts to
be dated prior to Ezekiel's activity, and others after it.[88] Fohrer
has suggested that a literary source or sources were used in
common. The original pre-exilic collection of laws has been lost,
but its essential contents are preserved both in the Holiness Code
and in Ezekiel's prophecy.[89]

The form-critical analyses of von Rad and Reventlow have
shown that the Holiness Code as a whole is the end-product of a
long development of tradition.[90] Like Deuteronomy it is presented as an address of Yahweh to Moses (Lev. 17.1). It concerns
the behaviour required of priests as well as lay people. But again
like Deuteronomy, the laws are explained (e.g. 17.5–7) and the
people are exhorted to keep them (e.g. 18.2–5). Von Rad suggested that the appropriate occasion for such teaching was
'community-instruction of a popular character carried out by the
Levites'.[91] The whole address is rounded off by the announcement
of blessings and curses that will fall upon those who keep, or fail
to keep, the laws (26.3–39).

In his further study *Wächter über Israel* Reventlow has examined
in detail the form-critical relationship between the book of
Ezekiel and the Holiness Code. He notes how frequently the

prophet appears to have derived from the tradition shared with the code both the reasons for, and the substance of, his prophecies of weal and woe.

On a number of occasions, phrases in Ezekiel which are paralleled in the Holiness Code are introduced by the conjunction *kī*, or some equivalent, which distinguishes them in Reventlow's opinion as quotations.[92] These may occur within personal addresses and involve a sudden change of speech from second to third person. For example, between the divine commission to perform an acted prophecy in Ezek. 5.1–4 and the explanation of the action in an address to Jerusalem (vv. 7ff.), there is a passage, also in the form of a divine address, but referring to Jerusalem and its inhabitants in the third person. The verses concerned (5–6) contain an accusation which is summarized in the closing words: '(for) they have rejected my judgments/ and have not walked in my statutes' ([*kī*] *bᵉmišpāṭay māʾāsū/wᵉḥuqqōtay lōʾ-hālᵉkū bāhem*). The first of these phrases is also found in Lev. 26.43b, while the latter is paralleled by the conditional – 'if you walk in my statutes' (*ʾim-bᵉḥuqqōtay tēlēkū*) – in Lev. 26.3a. Further use is made of traditional material in the accusations and prophecies of doom which follow. In Ezek. 5.10a both phrases – 'fathers shall eat (their) sons/and sons shall eat their fathers' (*ʾābōt yōʾkᵉlū bānīm[93]/ ūbānim yōʾkᵉlū ʾᵃbōtām*, 3+3) – are roughly paralleled in Lev. 26.29 – 'you shall eat the flesh of your sons/and you shall eat the flesh of your daughters' (*waʾᵃkaltem bᵉśar bᵉnēkem/ūbᵉśar bᵉnōtēkem tōʾkēlū*, 3+3). Both this example from a doom oracle and the previous example of an impersonally phrased accusation illustrate two points made by Reventlow. The first is that three-stress lines, typifying – as he supposes – so much of the material in Lev. 26,[94] also appear in Ezekiel. Furthermore, we should not conceive of the relationship between Ezekiel and the Holiness Code in terms of literary dependence on some hypothetical document. Synonymous expressions are often interchanged and verb forms altered. Prohibitions and conditional clauses may be rendered as accusations. Rather, the prophecy and the code are independent expressions of the same liturgy of covenant renewal.

Characteristic of Ezekiel's prophecy is the resumption (*die Wiederaufnahme*) of prophetic addresses after the words: 'and you will know that I am Yahweh'. That phrase is frequently followed by the preposition (*bᵉ*), with an infinitive and suffix. Some part of

the preceding oracle is repeated before the further development of
the prophetic address.[95] Thus in Ezek. 12.14–16, the prophecy
that Yahweh will 'scatter to the wind' all who help the prince of
Jerusalem (v. 14) is repeated in v. 15, in the synonymous phrases:
'when I disperse them among the nations and scatter them
through the countries'. That we have here again material tradi-
tionally associated with the curses of the covenant is apparent
from the parallel in Lev. 26.33: 'and I will scatter you among the
nations.'

Reventlow has also examined the prophecies of weal in Ezekiel
where parallels with the blessings in Leviticus 26 are in evidence.[96]
The 'historical surveys' of the prophecy also describe Israel's
apostasy in terms of the violation of covenant responsibilities. And
Ezekiel's declarations of sacral law reflect the form and content of
the laws in the Holiness Code. Thus appeals to covenant tradition
are found throughout the prophecy. We cannot deny all the
parallels between Ezekiel and the Holiness Code to the prophet
himself.[97] Even Fohrer's assignment of approximately half of
them to the editors of the prophecy[98] does not lessen the significance of the relationship.

S. R. Driver wrote of Ezekiel:

> He expresses himself in terms agreeing with the Law of Holiness in
> such a manner as only to be reasonably explained by the supposition
> that it formed a body of precepts with which he was familiar, and
> which he regarded as an authoritative basis of moral and religious
> life.[99]

Reventlow's study is valuable in that it has clarified the relationship between the prophecy and the law code. But Reventlow has
gone beyond the evidence in the conclusions he has drawn from
Ezekiel's numerous appeals to the covenant tradition. As in his
studies of Amos and Jeremiah,[100] he is concerned to identify the
sacral traditions to which the prophet alludes and, on account of
their setting (*Sitz im Leben*) in the cult to affirm the prophet's
'office' in the same institution.[101] But he takes little consideration
of the factors which distinguish the individual prophets, factors
which range from the character of their revelatory experiences to
the distinctive way each employs common traditions. In his
study of Ezekiel he has excluded from consideration 'all parts in
which adopted material of a profane character has displaced other

forms'.[102] Yet it is Ezekiel's use of such 'profane' material that sometimes distinguishes the prophecy markedly from other Old Testament literature.[103]

It also needs to be emphasized here – as numerous scholars have stressed – that the word of Yahweh which the prophets spoke was in every case a word addressed to men in specific situations. Reventlow himself affirms this,[104] but does not appear to take serious enough account of the fact. He has even rejected the possibility of distinguishing the two periods of Ezekiel's activity – before and after the destruction of Jerusalem.[105] All facets of the prophet's work are merged in the performance of a liturgy in which he repeats the time-honoured formulae affirming Israel's covenant responsibilities. In effect, we are not to take seriously the prophet's words about Yahweh's complete and utter rejection of his people. Nor does the 'new' act of Yahweh really inaugurate such a startlingly new possibility for Israel. But that is precisely what the author of Ezek. 16.60 understood when he asserted that Yahweh would remember the covenant of former days when he established an everlasting covenant with Israel. It is widely recognized that Ezek. 16.44–63 does not belong to the primary stratum of the Ezekiel tradition.[106] And the fact that v. 60 is part of a secondary element, affirming the significance of the former covenant, throws into contrast the prophet's own view that that covenant had, in the past, been continually dishonoured and had, therefore, been broken irrevocably. No reference is made to it when Ezekiel speaks of the future 'covenant of peace', for it was a thing of shame.

The real importance of what we have considered here is that Ezekiel's prophecies would have been recognized as plainly based on a tradition of covenant law. To the reason for this we shall give further thought in the concluding chapter.

E. *Conclusion*

Zimmerli has said that for all the 'evident contiguity' between the book of Ezekiel and earlier written prophecy, Ezekiel nevertheless stands in 'a quite special line' with the nationalistic prophets of northern Israel.[107] To affirm the contiguity with written prophecy he appeals to a section of Fohrer's *Die Hauptprobleme des Buches Ezechiel*,[108] and detailed consideration is given there to Ezekiel's relationship to Jeremiah and post-exilic prophecy – but not to Hosea.

We have attempted above to remedy this situation and suggest that Ezekiel's relationship to both Hosea and Jeremiah complements, rather than contrasts with, that to the Israelite pre-classical prophets. In no regard is this more clearly seen than in the attitude toward the covenant common to all these prophets. What Wolff terms 'the theme of (the people's) contempt for the divine covenant'[109] evident among the early prophetic circles of the north (I Kings 19.10, 14), is taken up in Hos.8.1 and is of fundamental importance in Jeremiah (cf. Jer. 31.31f.).

Although there was much misunderstanding and neglect of the covenant, both Deuteronomy and the Holiness Code represented the conditions for its maintenance. Ezekiel's relationship to Deuteronomy accentuates his concern to show that Yahweh's treatment of his people was the necessary outcome of their disobedience. But the covenant tradition he largely used was that shared with the Holiness Code.

IV

CONCLUSION

Ezekiel's was not the only prophetic voice to be heard in the early years of the sixth century BC. In attempting to account for the various relationships we have been examining, it is necessary first to consider Ezekiel's sense of divine authority in relation to the other prophets of his time. The possibility of attributing the relationship between Ezekiel and pre-classical prophecy to Ezekiel's followers is then considered. Finally assessments are made of Ezekiel's prophetic experience and of his place in the wider context of Israelite prophecy.

A. *The question of authority*

Jeremiah's letter to the exiles contained several references to prophets active in the exile community,[1] and Ezekiel (14.7–10) warned the exiles against inquiring of Yahweh through prophets. In his words against prophets generally, Ezekiel accused them of having failed to strengthen Israel's spiritual life (13.1–16). They are said to have prophesied without authority: 'They say, "says Yahweh", although I have not spoken' (13.7). Jeremiah's letter contains a similar criticism of the prophets in exile (29.9; cf. v. 31).

Such references emphasize how limited our knowledge of Israelite prophecy is. We are aware of the existence of some prophets – possibly great numbers of prophets – only by their opponents' disparaging words about them. Yet it is important to remember that there was this broad range of prophetic activity. For it was against such a background that Ezekiel had to assert his own authority and his efforts to do so have been significant in determining the character of his prophecy.

There is, for instance, the autobiographical prose of Ezekiel.

The extensive use of that style in Jeremiah has already been mentioned, and Bright has examined the incidence of auto-biographical material in other Old Testament prophecies.[2] Noting that its quantity appears to have increased in the course of time, he concludes that it is to be attributed to the prophets' need, in the face of increasing hostility, to authenticate their words by describing personally the experiences through which they were received. The autobiographical account of Micaiah's vision (I Kings 22.19–23) is certainly set in hostile circumstances, and the story of conflict between Amaziah and Amos over the latter's right to prophesy in Israel (Amos 7.10–17) is set within auto-biographical accounts of Amos' visions in 7.1–9.4. With the growing rift between prophets, greater emphasis would naturally have been placed on the right to speak in Yahweh's name. More-over, Ezekiel had from the outset to justify his prophesying in a foreign, and therefore unclean (4.13), land. He was listened to with interest, but also with incredulity (12.21–28; 33.30–33). The message he had to deliver was so harsh and so contrary to the expectations of his people. It must then have been imperative that he establish his authority by every possible means, including the narration of his experiences in autobiographical style.

The practice of dating prophecies is probably also related to the question of authority. Sometimes the dates in Ezekiel are attributed to a general interest in dates, exemplified in material from priestly authors elsewhere in the Old Testament. But their spasmodic appearance suggests instead that they indicate occasions which were of special significance to Ezekiel. As well as the occasion of his calling, and the time he heard the news of Jerusalem's fall, each major vision account of the book is dated.[3] Zimmerli's assertion that the tablets of Isa. 8.1f. and Hab. 2.2 were also likely to have been dated cannot be proved. But the Babylonian custom of dating to the day important written agreements, which Zimmerli also points out,[4] may well have influenced Ezekiel, as well as Haggai and Zechariah where more precisely dated prophecies are to be found. Like the tablets of Isaiah and Habakkuk, the dated pro-phecies of Ezekiel would thus have been intended to stand as evidence that the prophets had correctly described the course of events which Yahweh was bringing about. According to both Deut. 18.22 and Jer. 28.9, fulfilment was the ultimate criterion of 'true' prophecy.[5] The truth of Ezekiel's claim to be a messenger of Yahweh would be evident when what he had foreseen at specific times became realities apparent to all: 'then they will know that a prophet was in their midst' (Ezek. 33.33).

The prophetic form 'the word of divine self-demonstration',[6] with its recurrent 'and you (or, they) shall know that I am Yahweh', indicates concern that Yahweh himself should also be vindicated by the fulfilment of prophecy. But use of the covenant tradition common to Ezekiel and the Holiness Code provides the clearest evidence of the prophet's concern to authenticate his words. No one could say Ezekiel accused his people of acts they did not know were wrong. Nor were the threats he declared unfamiliar. It was because of Israel's departure from an agreement they had freely entered into that Yahweh was punishing them. Yahweh was no petulant tyrant but a God of justice, whose former acts of compassion had been forgotten and who would therefore correct his people according to the terms of his covenant with them. So Ezekiel proclaimed the justice of the exile and Jerusalem's destruction, elaborating the curses and – later for the most part – the blessings of the covenant, in the fashion of Jeremiah and other of his prophetic forbears.

This evidence of concern with prophetic authority is also important in explaining the appearance of the pre-classical prophetic traits in Ezekiel.

B. *The pre-classical prophetic traits and Ezekiel's tradition-circle*

Various theories have been proposed to account for the preservation and systematic ordering of Ezekiel's prophecy. It is generally agreed that the work, in so far as it represents the prophet's own words and account of his activity, has been elaborated in the course of transmission.[7] But there is wide diversity of opinion both as to the extent of such elaboration and as to whether it should be attributed to the prophet himself, or to disciples or later editors. Attention has been drawn in the course of this study to a number of points at which the primary tradition appears to have been elaborated by later hands. But our concern here is with the question of whether the similarities between the book of Ezekiel and the pre-classical prophetic narratives derived from Ezekiel or from those who preserved his prophecies.

Examples in Ezekiel of four of the topics discussed in ch. II – the hand of Yahweh, the concept of the spirit, the setting of a prophet's face toward the subjects of his utterances, and the elders sitting before a prophet in his house – are all found in the autobiographical narrative. As has just been pointed out, this material is likely to be part of Ezekiel's own account of his activity. Moreover, we have seen a number of ways in which the features of pre-classical prophecy found in Ezekiel appear to have been modified. 'Wind' rather than 'the spirit of Yahweh' conveys the prophet from place to place. A form of prophecy ensuring Israel's victory over her neighbours is employed to foretell and secure Israel's own overthrow, while the gesture of setting one's face toward people, used in ancient rites of cursing, is associated with Yahweh's activity in the sphere of worship.[8] Thus the pre-classical prophetic traits cannot be said to have been copied – as mere literary conventions or devices – from the pre-classical narratives. On the contrary, their appearance in modified forms suggests that they reflect Ezekiel's own prophetic experience and situation. When the pre-classical traits are used in secondary material, their significance may be misunderstood. For example, *rūaḥ* (rather than 'the hand of Yahweh') 'falls' upon Ezekiel and communicates a divine revelation (11.5).[9]

We know as little about the personal details of those who preserved Ezekiel's prophecy as we do about those who transmitted most of the other prophetic books. True, there are mentioned 'the sons of the prophets' associated with Elijah and Elisha, and 'the disciples' of Isaiah. These, like Baruch, probably assisted in recording and preserving the words of their great contemporaries. But it is interesting, in the light of the references to elders sitting before the prophets in II Kings 6 and Ezekiel, to consider the role of the eldership in the transmission of prophetic tradition.

Unfortunately, references to the activities of elders are relatively few and such material as concerns them has largely come by way of other circles – the priestly, the prophetic and the wise – whose interests were more directly concerned with their own activities. Noth has discerned the tendency to neglect the role of elders in the Exodus and Sinai events.[10] Yet the elders' extremely wide responsibility for the well-being of the people is still apparent in certain pentateuchal traditions of their legal, cultic and prophetic activities.[11] And it is probable that the elders' authority, although exercised to some extent throughout the period of the monarchies, became more significant among the exiles with the imprisonment of Jehoiachin.[12] Jeremiah, in his letter to the exiles, addressed the elders, along with the priests and prophets, as those worthy of special mention (29.1). And in Ezek. 7.26 it is 'the elders', rather than 'the wise' (cf. Jer. 18.18), whose inability to give counsel is anticipated, along with the failure of prophetic and priestly guidance.

The elders' part in maintaining the continuity of prophetic tradition, is most clearly illustrated in the remarkable passage Jer. 26.17ff. 'Certain elders of the land' rose in an assembly of the people and supported Jeremiah by referring to Micah's prophecy. Micah's unpopular intimation of Jerusalem's impending doom (3.12), which had contradicted the ambitious hopes of Israel's 'priests and prophets', was recalled not by the leaders of Israel's sacred institutions but by the common freemen of the land.

Thus we can recognize a wider dissemination of such tradition among the people generally than is sometimes implied by appeals to specific disciple groups or circles. This is a necessary corrective to the tendency to isolate the different tradition-circles at the expense of the organic whole. And it is possible, despite Ezekiel's hyperbolic condemnation of them, that 'certain elders of Israel' (14.1; 20.1) contributed significantly to the subsequent recollection and preservation of the prophet's words and activities.

C. *Ezekiel's prophetic experience*

From the book of Ezekiel we learn little about the background and circumstances of the prophet. We hear that he was married. But we know hardly anything of his origins and nothing of his fate. Even the conditions of his life in Babylon are obscure. Yet from his prophecies some aspects of his character can be discerned.

The general human potential for hallucinatory experience has given rise to the biblical and extra-biblical evidence already examined, which implies belief in translocation. Ezekiel's references to *rūaḥ* conveying him from place to place leave little doubt that he shared such experiences. His awareness of things beyond normal sense perception – when 'the hand of Yahweh' came upon him – confirms his extraordinary mental constitution. His prostration before the vision of the divine glory, his sitting 'overwhelmed' among the exiles (3.15), as well as his periods of dumbness and immobility (3.25f.; 4.4–8; 24.26f.),[13] are also significant indications of the prophet's character and temperament. Lindblom says: 'Neurotic and hysterical traits are more evident in (Ezekiel) than in the other prophets.'[14] Certainly Ezekiel's extreme emotional sensitivity, also exemplified by his reaction to the thought of his own defilement (4.14), is evident and helps account for his place in Israel's tradition of ecstatic prophecy.

In a study of prophecy in Mari, Huffmon notes that 'the modes of inspiration may fluctuate in popularity'. And in a suggestive parallel he comments: 'It may be that [in Israel] the turn to a more ecstatic prophecy in the time of Samuel, a turn then continued through the time of Elijah and Elisha, represents such a fluctuation.'[15] To broaden the perspective still further, the periodic resurgence of groups displaying ecstatic characteristics is a significant feature of church history.[16] Such a resurgence is evident at present in the widespread Pentecostal movement. People troubled by change and unable to accept contemporary explanations for it may find fresh purpose and energy by returning to a simpler outlook based on older values and profound emotional experiences.

Elijah and Elisha were active during the turbulent period of the Omrides and their successors. At the time of Samuel there was a crisis of leadership in the face of the Philistine threat. The parts played by Samuel and Elijah in restoring loyalty to the covenant have already been mentioned.[17] This is not to say that the groups led by Samuel, Elijah and Elisha were the only representatives of the ecstatic tradition or the only upholders of the covenant before Ezekiel. Ecstatic experience and the Sinai-Horeb covenant tradition are constant undercurrents in the history of Israel. But it is significant that figures representative of ecstatic prophecy should have played dominant roles in forcefully reaffirming the covenant precepts in times of crisis.[18] In Ezekiel's day a crisis of equal magnitude confronted Israel and he appears to have met it with similar resources.

The firm confidence that members of ecstatic movements may display derives from their intense experiences of divine power.[19] They tend also to see issues in unequivocal terms.[20] Such characteristics are shown by Ezekiel in his refusal to be intimidated by opposition and his outright condemnation of past and present Israelites. So firmly does he feel Yahweh's control that he finally attributes Israel's continuing sinfulness to Yahweh's deliberate misleading of his people by giving them evil laws (20.25f.). On the other hand, Ezekiel sees no difficulty in individuals making a complete break with their evil past (18.14, 21). And he envisages the ultimate renewal of the whole people. The gift to them of a new heart will be accompanied by their own divine encounter: for 'I will put my spirit within you' (37.14).

Apart from such personal and social factors, Ezekiel's physical situation – far from Jerusalem – predisposed him to express himself in ways similar to the pre-classical prophets. The phrase 'you shall know that I am Yahweh' could be uttered by prophets far from any cultic locale and even in the course of battle.[21] This removal from the normal cultic context of prophecy[22] is also emphasized by Ezekiel's prophesying in his own dwelling, with certain elders sitting before him.

That Ezekiel should have employed earlier forms of expression, even the language of the old schools of seers,[23] is not surprising. We have seen that he was concerned to authenticate his prophetic activities in the face of contemporary rivals. Recourse to older concepts and modes of expression would have helped establish him in the succession of earlier, and perhaps well-respected, prophets of crisis. His concern with authority was also a factor in his use of the covenant tradition common to the Holiness Code. Yet this last feature of his prophecy was also grounded in Ezekiel's own experience, or more specifically in his priestly heritage.[24] Although Ezekiel's words have, for the most part, the form of prophetic addresses, they also incorporate speech forms normally employed in priestly activity. Thus in ch. 14 the response to the elders who come to inquire of Yahweh through Ezekiel is clearly related to priestly declarations of sacred righteousness. The guilty are spoken of as 'any . . . who . . . (*'îš* *'îš''*)' – (vv. 4 and 7)[25] and conditions of guilt are put in the casuistic form typical of priestly law (v. 9). Also the punishment of the guilty is to be their exclusion from the people of Yahweh (vv. 8ff.). It is in this context too that 'the setting of the prophet's face toward the subjects of his prophecies' has special significance. For it was evidently related to that exclusion from divine favour which being 'cut off' from the community of the righteous involved (cf. Ezek. 14.8).

Reventlow's assessment of Ezekiel as one lacking 'spontaneity of spirit' and 'not a free religious individual, but one bound to the religious traditions of his people'[26] is hardly fair to the prophet. Reventlow is not alone in rejecting Wellhausen's portrayal of the classical prophets as 'awakened individuals' – 'always single, resting on nothing outside themselves'.[27] Yet, while Wellhausen's distinction between the independent spirits of the prophets and the rigid traditionalism of the priests may have been overdrawn, he was prepared to acknowledge that the prophets 'are not saying anything new: they are only proclaiming old truth'.[28] Or, as Ackroyd has put it:

> One might well imagine the horror of a prophet who was accused of innovation when he was in fact presenting what he knew to be the age-old realities of God as seen in the life and experience of his people.[29]

When the prophets declared divine judgment on their people it was not on account of an unwitting breach of their relationship with Yahweh, but on account of their deliberate neglect of the responsibilities which it involved.

Among the valuable contributions of Wellhausen to study of the prophets was his insistence that prophetic authority as a whole derived directly from Yahweh. Whether their guidance was sought (e.g. Jer. 21.1f.; Ezek. 20.1) or their words were unsolicited, the prophets did not regard what they said as the result of their own deliberations. They were messengers, the characteristic introduction of whose speech – 'thus said Yahweh' – indicated that they conveyed precisely the communications of one under whom the whole of Israel's life stood subject.[30] Thus it may be true that the foundation for the prophets' adoption and refashioning of the speech forms and motifs of their people's institutions, culture and environment was their awareness of their special office.[31] Freedom, by the very nature of their special charisma, from the strictures of a narrowly defined institutional role may have led them to express the word of Yahweh in the very forms used in those institutions and offices which had failed to honour his holy righteousness.

We must endeavour to hold in tension these two aspects of prophecy. There was on the one hand freedom to express personally communicated revelations which could cut across all the accepted customs and beliefs of Israel. But there was also an awareness that in the continuing prophetic representation of Yahweh's will was an underlying harmony which could be traced back to the obligations implicit in Yahweh's gracious election of his people. That Ezekiel *was* 'a great individualist and a hero of the spirit'[32] is clear despite the interpretation placed by Reventlow on his use of the covenant-festival tradition common to the Holiness Code.[33] There is no reason to deny Ezekiel's share in making faith possible for the exiles who 'pined away' (33.10) in their foreign dwelling. Nor can his use of the covenant blessings and curses in his verbal and acted prophecies be held part of a conventional representation of the covenant festival. The time for conventional ceremony was past. Ezekiel declared that the former covenant had been irrevocably broken and its curses were being made manifest. And he did so as a result of his personal encounter with Yahweh.

Again, the vision of Yahweh's glory in the plain and of its departing from Jerusalem must have involved for the prophet himself a radical reassessment of his former beliefs. For the location of the *kābōd* ('glory') at the Jerusalem sanctuary formed part of the traditions with which he was familiar. He interpreted his period of immobility as a sign of suffering for the sins of others (4.4–8).[34] This important concept was later developed in Second Isaiah's prophecy of the Suffering Servant (Isa. 52.13–53.12). His words regarding individual responsibility also indicate Ezekiel's independence of thought. From their use of the proverb: 'the fathers have eaten sour grapes, and the children's teeth are set on edge' (Ezek. 18.2), it seems the exiles came to accept that they were guilty in Yahweh's eyes (cf. 33.10). But they blamed their predecessors, perhaps on the grounds of threats such as that familiar from the decalogue: 'I . . . am a jealous God, visiting the iniquity of the fathers upon the children to the third and the fourth generation' (Ex. 20.5; Deut. 5.9). Although the principle of individual responsibility was recognized long before Ezekiel's period and is taken for granted in the early Book of the Covenant (Ex. 21–23), the prophet restated it in terms of the formulae used in priestly entrance liturgies – 'he shall surely live' or 'he shall surely die' for his own deeds (Ezek. 18.9, 13, etc.).[35] Once more, of course, this requires that account be taken of Ezekiel's priestly heritage. To underrate the influence of what is actually priestly tradition on the form and content of Ezekiel's prophecy is to ignore much that is distinctive in his work and to misconstrue the information it provides as to the nature of prophecy in general.

Ezekiel used a great variety of traditional concepts, popular tales and imagery in the service of his divine commission. Thus his work may best be understood in the context of the history of Israelite faith and thought. But this prophet, for whom even the death of his wife became a symbol of divine activity and who addressed himself to the complaints and distress of his fellow-exiles, impresses one with the depth of his personal convictions and his concern to apply his beliefs in his contemporary situation. His individuality is not to be denied because he reasserted what he regarded as the valid concepts of his religious heritage. Rather it is to be affirmed, because he stood against the contemporary currents of thought in his environment. And he did so with penetrating insight as to the meaning of the events that threatened to extinguish the distinctive faith of his people.

D.   *Ezekiel among the prophets*

It is reported in I Samuel (10.12; 19.24) that the saying became proverbial – 'Is Saul also among the prophets?' Not only in this century, but at least as early as the Council of Jamnia the same question might have been adapted – 'Is Ezekiel also among the prophets?' Has Ezekiel the right to be numbered among the great prophetic figures of Israel? Was Ezekiel a charlatan, hiding his priestly interests under a prophetic cloak? Or were the authors of the book of Ezekiel – writing in a period other than the early sixth century BC – using a fictitious hero as the vehicle of their ideas?

In a study which replies in the negative to these last two questions and affirms Ezekiel's just claim to rank among Israel's great prophets, it has seemed appropriate to use the title *Ezekiel Among the Prophets*, reminiscent as it is of the question asked by Saul's contemporaries. For it has been necessary to survey aspects of Israelite prophecy from its early stages among the wandering bands of *nᵉbî'îm* in order to clarify some of the less well-understood facets of the book of Ezekiel. And though it has been necessary to be selective, certain relationships have become apparent which mitigate the problems that the book poses.

Among these is the relationship to Jeremiah with the important similarities of style and imagery that have been outlined. It should be stressed again that Ezekiel, for all the parallels between his prophecy and that of Jeremiah, was no mere imitator of his contemporary. On the other hand, the similarities between the two, which go beyond what we might expect on account of the common influences of contemporary speech and thought forms, suggest that the younger prophet is to be regarded in a sense as a disciple, concerned to continue and extend his teacher's work among his fellow-exiles. Ezekiel was the heir to a long prophetic heritage, which in his period was expressed most forcefully and fully, so far as we know, in the prophecies of Jeremiah. It was for the continuation of that heritage that Ezekiel knew himself to be authorized and he strove to maintain it. Thus it is only to be expected that his prophecies should reflect Jeremiah's so clearly, even though there were important differences between the situations to which the prophets addressed themselves.

Also, there is the relationship between Ezekiel and the pre-classical prophets, with their appeals to 'the hand of Yahweh' and 'the spirit' as mediums of inspiration and translocation, and the other common characteristics we have examined that were suitable to Ezekiel's situation in exile. The similarities are numerous and so rarely paralleled in an exact sense in pre-exilic canonical prophecy as to confirm that a distinct strand of prophetic tradition is involved.

The question then arises, of course, whether we are to associate Ezekiel with a distinctive type of prophetic activity, perhaps with that of the $n^eb\bar{i}'\bar{i}m$, regarded as a class of official 'cult prophets'. Such is the view of Reventlow,[36] and Zimmerli has expressed himself similarly.[37] This is a complex issue. How much more we would like to know about cult prophets. How much we would like to know the nature of the 'spiritual exercises' they are supposed to have undertaken to attain ecstatic experience.[38] It is hardly satisfactory in our present state of knowledge to distinguish Ezekiel and the pre-classical prophets as 'cult prophets'. For while there are likely to have been real distinctions between Israel's prophets in their modes of activity,[39] the relationship of the pre-exilic canonical prophets to the cult is still an open question. And as more is understood of their use of cultic forms and the place of prophecy in the cult, it is becoming increasingly difficult to dissociate their activity firmly from the sphere of worship. Gunneweg has concluded that all prophets were *nᵉbi'im* and the classical prophets can only be distinguished tentatively as those who undertook their cultic responsibilities with radical seriousness.[40] We have also noted above the difficulty of distinguishing between so-called 'true' and 'false' prophets.[41] Attempts to distinguish them according to their manner of inspiration or whether they were active in the cult seem misdirected. Mowinckel was much closer to the point when he said that moral and religious criteria, and zeal for Yahweh's honour, came to typify classical prophecy.[42] It was the content of their messages that was important, not the way the prophets received them nor the official functions of the prophets.

In his study of falsehood in Jeremiah, Overholt has shown the significance of Jeremiah's attitude toward the tradition of Zion's inviolability. It was the prophet's independent stance in regard to the promise of God's care for Zion that enabled him to criticize the hopes of those who could not see beyond promises of continued security. The ideals of national sovereignty and peace were as important in that day as they are in our own. But Jeremiah saw Yahweh's freedom to act contrary to his earlier assurances because of his people's disobedience.[43] Some prophets proclaimed 'peace' without sufficient attention to the corresponding demand for righteousness in social and religious life. Perhaps the popularity of comfortable words overwhelmed their judgment of the political situation. Or it may have been that the genuine concern of some prophets to affirm Yahweh's continuing care for his people blinded them to the conditional nature of the agreement between them: '*If* you will obey my voice and keep my covenant, you shall be my own possession among all peoples' (Ex. 19.5).

Ezekiel was aware of the traditions of Zion and the promises to the royal house which dominated the thought of most Judeans. Both traditions are affirmed in his prophecies of restoration (the former in 43.1–12; the latter in 34.23f.; 37.22–24). But Ezekiel stood much closer to the tradition which held the Sinai/Horeb covenant to be the primary element of Israel's faith.[44] Advocates of this tradition had formerly opposed both cult and king when they failed to measure up to the standards of the covenant.[45] The combination of concern for the Sinai/Horeb covenant and the ecstatic experience of its prophetic advocates are the outstanding features of the tradition common to Ezekiel and the pre-classical prophets that we have been examining.

At the outset of this study it was said that there were two fundamental ways in which pre-classical prophecy could have influenced Ezekiel's work. The first was that of simple literary dependence of the later prophet on the records of his predecessors. The second was that pre-classical prophetic concepts persisted as viable expressions of prophetic experience among some circles of Israelites. With regard to the second possibility, we can no more deny than affirm the existence of such circles, although we may assume some neglect of the pre-classical traits in the intervening period.[46] On the other hand, the similarities between the book of Ezekiel and the prophetic narratives of I Kings 17ff. suggest that Ezekiel himself was familiar with that pre-classical material in something like its present form. But there is no need to assert his direct literary dependence – that he had before him in exile a copy of the early narratives. As with his knowledge of Jeremiah's prophecies,[47] oral reports of the pre-classical narratives may have been the source of Ezekiel's knowledge of them. The accessibility of the pre-classical narratives is not in question. They were available to the authors of the Deuteronomic history (Deuteronomy to Kings), who were the chief heirs of the opposition group of prophets and Levites in northern Israel.

This alliance of Levitical and prophetic interests, to which we have already referred,[48] was not only of significance for preserving the pre-classical prophetic narratives. It also appears to have prompted new emphases in prophetic activity. There is a pronounced community of thought between the Deuteronomists and Jeremiah,[49] which is particularly evident in the exhortatory tone of Jeremiah's prose words.[50] E. W. Nicholson has attributed those prose words, which he terms 'preaching to the exiles', to the Deuteronomic circle.[51] But it is apparent from Ezekiel that prophets themselves could deliver exhortations based on prophecies of threat or promise. Numerous passages appear as thinly veiled sermons rather than as oracles. Ezekiel 20.1–31 admonishes the exiles for their idolatry, reminding them of the long history of their forefathers' disobedience and its terrible consequences. Chapter 18 exhorts the exiles to find life by obeying Yahweh's statutes and ordinances. The broad parallels between these passages and Deuteronomy and the Holiness Code, with their admonitions based on Yahweh's gracious acts and their exhortations to observe the law, are obvious.

The pastoral role Ezekiel was called to assume as Israel's watchman (3.16–21; 33.1–20) was one outcome of the alliance of prophets and Levites. With his prophetic task of announcing Yahweh's intentions he was to combine that of personally exhorting his people to right living. He was to help them understand and apply the law to their everyday lives. Deuteronomy 33.10 regards such instruction as the first priority of the Levites and it is likely to have been undertaken by them in the pre-exilic period.[52] The Chronicler acknowledges the Levites' role as expositors of the law in the time of Ezra (Neh. 8.7f.).

The opposite – but equally natural – outcome of the alliance of Levites and prophets is also seen in the work of the Chronicler. He attributes to Levites prophetic activity in the course of worship (I Chron. 25.1ff.; II Chron. 20.14ff.), probably reflecting the adoption of prophetic roles by the Levitical singers of the second temple.

Study of Ezekiel's place in prophetic tradition thus indicates that prophecy as a whole should not be isolated in the fashion of earlier Old Testament scholarship. It calls attention to the interdependence of members of varied vocations – including laymen and kings[53] – in preserving and fostering knowledge of the relationship between Yahweh and his people. It reminds us also of the variety of prophetic activity there was in Israel. We have traced one strand of this activity from Ezekiel back to its earliest known representatives. This distinctive tradition combined emphasis on whole-hearted response to the Sinai/Horeb covenant with intense enthusiasm, expressed in ecstatic behaviour, on the part of the prophetic advocates of the covenant.

In his attempt to come to terms with the tragic fate of his people, Ezekiel drew on and developed many other strands of Israelite tradition. His work presents many contrasts, particularly in his portrayal of Yahweh as holy, yet deeply concerned for individuals; as demanding, yet gracious in his care for the outcast and defenceless. And if the prophetic message of judgment reaches unparalleled intensity in Ezekiel, so too does the message of forgiveness and new hope. It is a hope that the lives of all God's people will find new power and purpose through his spirit. So those who share Ezekiel's anger at injustices today should also share his hope for tomorrow. And those who find in his words deserved condemnation of our broken human relationships may also find encouragement in their efforts to realize the healing and peace[54] that God wills for us.

NOTES

I. INTRODUCTION

1. W. Zimmerli, *Ezechiel* (BKAT 13), 1955–69; ET in preparation.
2. *VT* 15 (1965), pp. 515ff.
3. More detailed surveys can be found in a number of readily accessible works such as: H. H. Rowley, 'The Book of Ezekiel in Modern Study', *BJRL* 36, 1953–4, pp. 146ff. = *Men of God*, London 1963, pp. 169ff.; H. G. May, 'Ezekiel', *IB* 6, pp. 41ff.; O. Eissfeldt, *The Old Testament: an Introduction*, ET Oxford 1965, pp. 367ff.; G. Fohrer, *Introduction to the Old Testament*, ET London 1970, pp. 403ff.
4. S. R. Driver, *An Introduction to the Literature of the Old Testament*, Edinburgh ⁹1913, p. 279.
5. G. Hölscher, *Hesekiel. Der Dichter und das Buch* (BZAW 39), 1924.
6. C. C. Torrey, *Pseudo-Ezekiel and the Original Prophecy*, New Haven 1930.
7. James Smith, *The Book of the Prophet Ezekiel*, London 1931.
8. V. Herntrich, *Ezechielprobleme* (BZAW 61), 1932.
9. E.g. A. Bertholet, *Hesekiel* (HAT 13), 1936; H. Wheeler Robinson, *Two Hebrew Prophets: Studies in Hosea and Ezekiel*, London 1948; P. Auvray, 'Le problème historique du livre d'Ézéchiel', *RB* 55, 1948, pp. 503ff.; et al.
10. G. A. Cooke, *Ezekiel* (ICC), 1936.
11. C. G. Howie, *The Date and Composition of Ezekiel* (*JBL* Monograph Series 4), 1950.
12. G. Fohrer, 'Die Glossen im Buche Ezechiel', *ZAW* 63, 1951, pp. 33ff.; *Die Hauptprobleme des Buches Ezechiel* (BZAW 72), 1952, and subsequently *Ezechiel* (HAT 13), 1955.
13. W. Zimmerli, *Ezechiel* (BKAT) and articles in *Gottes Offenbarung: Gesammelte Aufsätze* (ThB 19), 1963.
14. K. von Rabenau, 'Die Entstehung des Buches Ezechiel in formgeschichtlicher Sicht', *WZ Halle* 5, 1955–6, pp. 659ff.; 'Die Form des Rätsels im Buche Hesekiel', *WZ Halle* 7, 1957–8, pp. 1055ff.; 'Das prophetische Zukunftswort im Buch Hesekiel', in *Studien zur Theologie der alttestamentlichen Überlieferungen: Festschrift G. von Rad*, ed. R. Rendtorff and K. Koch, Neukirchen 1961, pp. 61ff.
15. W. Eichrodt, *Der Prophet Hesekiel* (ATD) 1959–66; ET *Ezekiel* (OTL), 1970.
16. J. W. Wevers, *Ezekiel* (New Century Bible, London 1969).
17. See too the shorter commentaries of D. M. G. Stalker, *Ezekiel* (Torch Bible Commentaries), London 1968; K. W. Carley, *Ezekiel* (Cambridge Bible), Cambridge 1974.

18. See H. F. Hahn, *The Old Testament in Modern Research*, London 1956, Philadelphia ²1966, pp. 119ff.; K. Koch, *The Growth of the Biblical Tradition*, ET London 1969; G. M. Tucker, *Form Criticism of the Old Testament*, Philadelphia 1971.

19. H. Gunkel's programme is outlined in 'Die israelitische Literatur', in *Die Kultur der Gegenwart* 7, ed. P. Hinneberg, Berlin 1906, §1, pp. 51ff.

20. On contemporary speech and literary convention, see M. A. K. Halliday et al., *The Linguistic Sciences and Language Teaching*, London 1964, esp. pp. 75–110.

21. For consideration of the theses of Nyberg, Birkeland, Engnell and Nielsen, see the more balanced assessments of S. Mowinckel, *Prophecy and Tradition* (ANVAO 3), 1946, pp. 15ff., and G. Widengren, *Literary and Psychological Aspects of the Hebrew Prophets* (UUå 10), 1948, pp. 1ff.

22. In particular the Priestly, Deuteronomic and various prophetic circles.

23. For the principal literary forms found in prophecy see Muilenburg, 'Old Testament Prophecy' in *Peake's Commentary on the Bible*, 2nd edn, ed. M. Black and H. H. Rowley, London and Edinburgh 1962, §413; and C. Westermann, *Basic Forms of Prophetic Speech*, ET London 1967.

24. G. Fohrer, 'Remarks on the Modern Interpretation of the Prophets', *JBL* 80, 1961, pp. 311ff.; see also J. Muilenburg, 'Form Criticism and Beyond', *JBL* 88, 1969, pp. 1ff.; R. Knierim, 'Old Testament Form Criticism Reconsidered', *Interpr.* 27, 1973, pp. 435ff.

25. See too J. Lindblom, p. 197 of 'Wisdom in the Old Testament Prophets', *SVT* 3 (1955), pp. 192ff.; though cf. R. B. Y. Scott, p. 37 of 'The Study of the Wisdom Literature', *Interpr.* 24 (1970), pp. 20ff.

26. Gunkel, p. 66 of 'Fundamental Problems of Hebrew Literary History', in *What Remains of the Old Testament and other essays*, ET London 1928, pp. 57ff.; and cf. Mowinckel, *IDB* 3, s.v. 'Literature', p. 143a.

27. Gunkel, op. cit., p. 65.

28. Amos 4.4–5; 5.4–5, 21–24; see J. Begrich, 'Die priesterliche Tora' in *Werden und Wesen des Alten Testaments* (BZAW 66), 1936, pp. 63ff.

29. See G. von Rad, '"Righteousness" and "Life" in the Cultic Language of the Psalms' (1950), in *The Problem of the Hexateuch and other essays*, ET Edinburgh and London 1966, pp. 243ff.; Zimmerli, '"Leben" und "Tod" im Buche des Propheten Ezechiel' (1957), in *Gottes Offenbarung*, pp. 178ff.

30. G. Fohrer, 'Tradition und Interpretation im Alten Testament', *ZAW* 73, 1961, pp. 1ff.

31. D. R. Jones, 'The Traditio of the Oracles of Isaiah of Jerusalem', *ZAW* 67 (1955), pp. 226ff.

32. Ibid., p. 227; cf. Fohrer, *Introduction*, p. 30.

33. See Koch, *The Growth of the Biblical Tradition*, pp. 56f., although Koch uses the term 'motif' in a more restricted sense as 'the smallest element which goes into the construction of a tradition'. S. Talmon dissociates 'form-' and 'motif-analysis' too firmly, although he has offered a useful definition of the term 'motif' on pp. 38f. of 'The "Desert Motif" in the Bible and in the Qumran Literature', in *Biblical Motifs*, ed. A. Altmann, Cambridge, Mass., 1966, pp. 31ff.

34. A. Jirku, *Die älteste Geschichte Israels im Rahmen lehrhafter Darstellungen*, Leipzig 1917.

35. J. Lindblom, p. 101 of 'Zur Frage des kanaanäischen Ursprungs des altisraelitischen Prophetismus', in *Festschrift O. Eissfeldt* (BZAW 77), 1958, pp. 89ff.

36. S. Mowinckel, 'The "Spirit" and the "Word" in the Pre-exilic Reforming Prophets', *JBL* 53, 1934, pp. 199ff.; supplemented by 'Postscript', *JBL* 56, 1937, pp. 261ff.

37. N. Porteous, p. 227 of 'Prophecy', in *Record and Revelation. Essays on the Old Testament by Members of the Society for Old Testament Study*, ed. H. Wheeler Robinson, Oxford 1938, pp. 216ff.

38. J. Skinner, *Prophecy and Religion. Studies in the Life of Jeremiah* (Cambridge, 1922), p. 4 n. 1.

39. H. H. Rowley, p. 105 of 'The Nature of Old Testament Prophecy in the Light of Recent Study', in *The Servant of the Lord*, Oxford, [2]1965, pp. 97ff.

40. See C. F. Burney, *Notes on the Hebrew Text of the Books of Kings*, Oxford 1903, pp. 208f.; S. R. Driver, *Introduction*, p. 188 n. 1; also A. Šanda, *Die Bücher der Könige* (EH), 1911–12, I, pp. 455, 507f.; II, pp. 79f., 84, 122, et al.

41. See again Šanda, in loc.; also M. Wagner, *Die lexikalischen und grammatikalischen Aramaismen im alttestamentlichen Hebräisch* (BZAW 96), 1966, esp. p. 144.

42. I Kings 20.1–34; 22.1–37; II Kings 3.4ff.; 9.1–10.27.

43. See e.g. Eissfeldt, *Introduction*, p. 48; Mowinckel, pp. 18f. of 'Israelite Historiography', *ASTI* 2, 1963, pp. 4ff.

44. I Kings 18–19, 21; II Kings 5; 6.8–7.20; 8.7–15; 13.14–19.

45. J. Gray, *I & II Kings* (OTL), [2]1970, pp. 466, 470; Šanda, op. cit., II, p. 86.

46. Admittedly, the literary coherence has been imposed on originally independent narratives (see Eissfeldt, *Introduction*, p. 291; cf. Alt, pp. 135f. of 'Das Gottesurteil auf dem Karmel' [1935], in *KS* II, [2]1959, pp. 135ff.).

47. So too, with the Christian saints and apostles.

48. I.e. II Kings 2; 4.38–44; 6.1–7; 13.20f.

49. II. 4.1–37; 5; 6.8–7.20; cf. Šanda, op. cit., II, pp. 78f., 86f.

50. J. A. Montgomery, *Kings* (ICC), 1951, ed. H. S. Gehman, pp. 40 n. 1, and 369f.

51. Cf. Eissfeldt, op. cit., p. 148.

52. See Eissfeldt, ibid; von Rad, *Old Testament Theology* II, ET Edinburgh and London, 1965, p. 34; although some scholars are inclined to accept the few oracles we have as genuine (see e.g. van der Ploeg, who refers specifically to II Kings 3.16–19, p. 35 of 'Le rôle de la tradition orale dans la transmission du texte de l'Ancien Testament', *RB* 54, 1947, pp. 5ff.).

53. G. R. Driver, *Semitic Writing from Pictograph to Alphabet* (Schweich Lectures 1944), London [2]1954, pp. 88f.

54. H. W. Wolff, 'Hoseas geistige Heimat', *ThLZ* 81, 1956, cols 83ff.= *Gesammelte Studien zum Alten Testament* (ThB 22), 1964, pp. 232ff.

55. Retaining the MT of Hos. 4.5ab (prophets 'also stumble' with priests) with P. R. Ackroyd, 'Hosea', *Peake's Commentary*, 2nd edn, ed. Black and Rowley, §533b, et al.

56. Hos. 8.5f.; 10.5; 13.2.
57. Ex. 32.25–29; Deut. 33.9–10. See A. H. J. Gunneweg, *Leviten und Priester* (FRLANT 89), 1965, pt I.A, §§4–5.
58. See H. W. Wolff, *Hosea* (BKAT 14/1), 1961, p. xxvi.
59. As E. W. Nicholson asserts – *Deuteronomy and Tradition*, Oxford 1967, pp. 73ff. and esp. p. 79.
60. Deut. 9.7–10.11; esp. 10.8f.
61. A. H. J. Gunneweg, *Mündliche und schriftliche Tradition der vorexilischen Prophetenbücher* (FRLANT 73), 1959, p. 78.
62. E. Jacob, *La tradition historique en Israël* (Études theologiques et religieuses), Montpellier 1946, p. 41.
63. R. E. Clements, 'Deuteronomy and the Jerusalem Cult Tradition', *VT* 15, 1965, p. 300ff.; *God and Temple*, Oxford 1965, pp. 79ff.
64. A. C. Welch, *The Code of Deuteronomy*, London 1924; A. Alt, 'Die Heimat des Deuteronomiums' (1953) in *KS* II, pp. 250ff.; et al.
65. Jer. 1.1; cf. I Kings 2.26f. On Abiathar's Levitical origins see R. de Vaux, *Ancient Israel: Its Life and Institutions*, ET London 1961, pp. 359f., 372ff.

II. EZEKIEL AND PRE-CLASSICAL PROPHECY

1. 1.3; 3.14, 22; 8.1; 33.22; 37.1; 40.1.
2. Zimmerli, *Ezechiel* (BKAT), p. 47.
3. Deut. 4.34; 5.15; 7.19; 11.2; 26.8.
4. See e.g. Ezek. 33.22; and C. H. Cornill, *Das Buch des Propheten Ezechiel*, Leipzig 1886, p. 9.
5. Zimmerli, 'The Special Character of Ezekiel's Prophecy', *VT* 15, 1965, p. 517.
6. See Y. Yadin, *The Art of Warfare in Biblical Lands*, London 1963, pp. 284f.
7. P. W. Harrison, *The Arab at Home*, London 1924, p. 2.
8. J. Gray, *Kings* (OTL), p. 404.
9. *GK*, §111 l.
10. Reading *'emeth* adverbially, with Gray, op. cit., p. 383.
11. LXX has the verb (ἐξ-)αἴρειν or ἀναλαμβάνειν in I Kings 18.12; II. 2.16; Ezek. 3.12; etc.
12. See Liddell and Scott, *A Greek-English Lexicon*, new (9th) edn, ed. H. S. Jones and R. McKenzie, Oxford, 1940, s.v. ἁρπάζω.
13. See pp. 34ff.
14. Treating *wᵉhāyā*, in parenthesis, as a frequentative perfect consecutive, 'representing actions which have continued or been repeated in the past' (*GK* §112e); so Montgomery, *Kings* (ICC), pp. 361, 365; Gray, op. cit., p. 483, note f.
15. See e.g. W. W. Sargant, *Battle for the Mind: a Physiology of Conversion and Brain-washing*, London ²1959.
16. *Body and Mind: Readings in Philosophy*, ed. G. N. A. Vesey, London 1964.

17. W. Grey Walter, *The Living Brain*, Harmondsworth ²1961, pp. 11f.
18. G. Révész, *Introduction to the Psychology of Music*, ET London 1953, p. 35.
19. Walter, op. cit., pp. 60–75.
20. See Sargant, who understands the mechanism in terms of the overburdening and collapse of the mental constitution (op. cit., pp. 54ff., etc.), and I. Ramage, who, following more orthodox psychoanalytic theory, believes that music etc. may lower the capacity of the mind to repress emotions (*Battle for the Free Mind*, London 1967, pp. 47ff. etc.).
21. On this see H. Kohut and S. Levarie, 'On the Enjoyment of Listening to Music', *Psychoanalytic Quarterly* 19, 1950, pp. 64ff., summarized in *Annual Survey of Psychoanalysis* (*ASP*) 1, New York 1950, pp. 127ff., 372f.; and H. Kohut, 'The Psychological Significance of Musical Activity', *Music Therapy* 1,1951, pp. 151ff., summarized *ASP* 2, 1951, pp. 480ff.
22. C. Sachs, *A Short History of World Music*, London ²1956, p. 18; A. Z. Idelsohn, *Jewish Music in its Historical Development*, New York ²1948, p. 111.
23. For such beliefs among Christian Pentecostal groups (where music plays an important role), see J. L. Sherrill, *They Speak with Other Tongues*, London 1965, pp. 134ff.
24. Sachs, op. cit., p. 3; M. Schneider, 'Primitive Music', in *New Oxford History of Music* I, *Ancient and Oriental Music*, ed. E. Wellesz, London 1957, pp. 3ff.; L. B. Glick, 'Musical Instruments in Ritual', in *Encyclopaedia of Papua and New Guinea* II, ed. P. Ryan, Melbourne 1972, pp. 821f.
25. E.g. blasts from rams' horns play a part in the conquest of Jericho (Josh. 6); and the same instruments are used to call Yahweh's attention to his warriors (Num. 10.9). Aaron's ephod is trimmed with bells, for religious ministrants needed protection from the evil spirits which frequented sanctuaries and thresholds (Ex. 28.33–35). Cf. C. Sachs, *The History of Musical Instruments*, New York 1940, esp. pp. 105–27; Idelsohn, op. cit., p. 15.
26. A. W. Ambros, *Geschichte der Musik*, Breslau 1862, quoted by A. M. Rothmüller, *The Music of the Jews: an Historical Appreciation*, ET London 1953, p. 24.
27. Noting the parallels with the psalms of lamentation, H. Reventlow regards the 'confessions' as public laments made on behalf of the faithful against those who threatened their well-being – *Liturgie und prophetisches Ich bei Jeremia*, Gütersloh 1963. But just as it was possible for a national psalm to be attributed to Hannah (I Sam. 2.1–10), individuals could adopt elements of cultic laments to bewail their own fate. See also J. Bright, 'Jeremiah's Complaints: Liturgy, or Expressions of Personal Distress?' in *Proclamation and Presence*, ed. J. I. Durham and J. R. Porter, London 1970, pp. 189ff.
28. Skinner, *Prophecy and Religion*, pp. 201ff.; J. P. Hyatt, 'Jeremiah', IB 5, pp. 782f.
29. Cf. W. Baumgartner, *Die Klagegedichte des Jeremia* (BZAW 32), 1917, pp. 36f.
30. See p. 13 above.
31. Understanding the intransitive *yāšabtī* in the sense of the English present tense – thus, 'I sit (alone)' (see *GK*, §106g).
32. *ḥezqā* is understood as a noun by both *BDB* and *KBL*, (s.v., *ḥzq*). *GK*

§45d and *BL* §49i regard it as a modified form of the infinitive construct from *ḥzq*.

33. Or, 'turned me aside, from walking . . .', reading *wayᵉsirēnī* for *wᵉyissᵉrēnī* or *wᵉyissᵉranī*, on the analogy of Deut. 7.4; so G. B. Gray, *Isaiah* 1–39 (ICC), 1912, pp. 151ff.

34. B. Duhm, *Das Buch Jesaia* (HK), ⁴1922, pp. 82f.; G. B. Gray, op. cit.

35. Omitting the clause 'with a strong hand he will send them out, yea . . .'. This appears to be a secondary variant, repeating the word *šallaḥ* (pi.) of 5.1; so Noth, *Exodus*, ET (OTL), 1962, p. 56.

36. '*Mit Gewalt*', *Exodus* (ATD), 1958, pp. 35, 41.

37. *bᵉyād ḥᵃzāqā*, Deut. 6.21 et al. (cf. n. 3 above). *bᵉḥōzeq yād*, Ex. 13.3, 14,16. Ex. 13.1–16 is attributed to the Deuteronomists by Noth, following Wellhausen et al.

38. R. B. Y. Scott, 'Isaiah 1–39', *IB* 5, p. 226.

39. Literally, 'who will not prophesy?'

40. Scott, loc. cit.

41. Cf. Isa. 7.7; 10.24; 18.4; etc.

42. Ezek. 1.12, 20; cf. 1.21; 10.17.

43. Ezek. 2.2; 3.24.

44. Ezek. 36.27; 37.14; 39.29; cf. 11.19; 36.26.

45. Ezek. 3.12, 14; 8.3; 11.1, 24; 43.5; cf. 37.1; 40.1ff.

46. G. von Rad, *Old Testament Theology* I, ET Edinburgh 1962, p. 97.

47. S. Mowinckel, 'The "Spirit" and the "Word"', *JBL* 53, 1934, pp. 199ff.

48. Von Rad, *Old Testament Theology* II, ET Edinburgh 1965, pp. 56f.

49. Y. Kaufmann, *The Religion of Israel*, ET London 1961, pp. 97ff.

50. I Chron. 12.18; II Chron. 15.1ff.; 20.14ff.; Neh. 9.30.

51. Cf. J. Lindblom, *Prophecy in Ancient Israel*, Oxford 1962, pp. 413f.; W. Eichrodt, *Theology of the Old Testament* I, ET (OTL), 1961, pp. 406ff.

52. Zimmerli, *Ezechiel* (BKAT), p. 244.

53. A. R. Johnson, *The One and the Many in the Israelite Conception of God*, Cardiff ²1961, pp. 15ff.; cf. J. Gray, *Kings* (OTL), pp. 463f.

54. So Johnson, *The Vitality of the Individual in the Thought of Ancient Israel*, Cardiff ²1964, pp. 25ff.

55. P. Humbert, *Problèmes du livre d'Habacuc* (Mémoires de l'Université de Neuchâtel 18), Neuchâtel 1944, pp. 13ff., 38f., 283.

56. M. Buber, *The Prophetic Faith*, ET New York 1949, pp. 63f.

57. Against Mowinckel, 'The "Spirit" and the "Word"', *JBL* 53, 1934, p. 199.

58. Von Rad is justifiably more cautious in associating prophecy and holy war; see *Der heilige Krieg im alten Israel* (AThANT 20), 1951, pp. 50ff.; see also the study of R. Bach, *Die Aufforderungen zur Flucht und zum Kampf im alttestamentlichen Prophetenspruch* (WMANT 9), 1962, on the development of the role of prophets in holy war.

59. Lindblom, *Prophecy in Ancient Israel*, p. 177 n. 112.

60. Cf. T. H. Robinson and F. Horst, *Die zwölf kleinen Propheten* (HAT 14), 1938, pp. 36f.; A. Weiser, *Das Buch der zwölf kleinen Propheten* I (ATD 24), ³1959, p. 73.

61. Neither metrical nor syntactical grounds are agreed on generally as bases for deleting the words 'the spirit of Yahweh' in Micah 3.8. The weight of recent opinion favours their retention (see R. E. Wolfe, 'Micah', *IB* 6, p.919; Weiser, op. cit., pp.256ff.; Lindblom, op. cit., p.175 n.109). And certainly, in the absence of more decisive grounds for emendation within the prophecy, to retain the phrase is to treat the text more fairly.

62. As Mowinckel maintains; so also Zimmerli, 'The Special Character of Ezekiel's Prophecy', *VT* 15, 1965, p.517.

63. Widengren, *Literary and Psychological Aspects*, pp.94ff.

64. Acts 5.1–16; 8.39; 10.9–20; etc.

65. M. Eliade, *Myths, Dreams and Mysteries*, ET London ²1968, p.88.

66. 'To lift, bear, or take away', as in I Kings 18.12; II Kings 2.16.

67. Ezek.3.12, 14; 8.3; 11.1, 24; 43.5.

68. Ezek.3.14; 8.1.

69. See ch.I n.9 above.

70. The relevant editorial passages isolated by Herntrich in *Ezechielprobleme* were: the references to the exiles and Chaldaea in 1.1–3; the commission and removal back to Tel-abib in 3.10–15; the removal to the temple and round about it in 8.2–4; 11.1, 22–25; and the delay in the fugitive's arrival in 33.21f. (cf.24.25f.). The vision of chs 40–48, like the opening vision (1.1–28), is entirely from the editor. But his supposed aim of encouraging the exiles could have been as well achieved without the fiction of an exilic setting for the prophecies against Jerusalem and Judah.

71. For example, 'the hand' appears alone in 1.3; 33.22; *rūaḥ* alone in 2.2; 11.1; 43.5.

72. On 11.5 see p.25 above. Furthermore, the Greek equivalent of 'Yahweh' (11.5) does not appear in all LXX mss. That 'the spirit' (11.24a) should be said to bring Ezekiel 'in the vision, *by the spirit*' (11.24b) emphasizes excessively the activity of the spirit, and this is the only reference in Ezekiel to 'the spirit of God'. Probably 11.24 once read 'in visions of God'.

73. So *BDB*, s.v. *rūaḥ*; H. G. May, '*Ezekiel*', *IB* 6, p.77; et al.

74. See *KBL* s.v. *rūaḥ* and Baumgärtel in *TDNT* 6 s.v. πνεῦμα, pp.359ff.; also D. Lys, '*Rûaḥ*'. *Le Souffle dans l'Ancien Testament* (Études d'histoire et de philosophie religieuses 56), Paris 1962; Zimmerli, *Ezechiel* (BKAT), Excurs 3, pp.1262ff.

75. P. Volz, *Der Geist Gottes und die verwandten Erscheinungen im Alten Testament und im anschliessenden Judentum*, Tübingen 1910.

76. L. Dürr, *Die Stellung des Propheten Ezechiel in der israelitisch-jüdischen Apocalyptik*, Münster 1923, p.24 n.2.

77. Eichrodt, *Theology of the Old Testament* I, p.308 n.1.

78. 'The spirit of Yahweh' may be indicated in the throne vision by the article prefixed to *rūaḥ* (1.12, 20), which apparently constituted the motive power for 'the wheels' and the life principle of 'the living creatures'.

79. So Amos 4.13; Jer.10.13; cf. H. Wheeler Robinson, *Two Hebrew Prophets*, p.90; Eichrodt, *Theology of the Old Testament* II, ET (OTL), 1967, pp.46f. 'Wind' in the strict sense (*seʿārā*) was known in prophetic tradition as an instrument of translocation, as in the narrative of Elijah's translation to heaven (II Kings 2.11, cf. I Enoch referred to below).

80. Dürr (following Cornill), deletes the *yhwh* of *bᵉrūaḥ yhwh* in 37.1. It is true that *rūaḥ* is usually the subject of the verb referring to Ezekiel's removal. But that the second *yhwh* of the verse is retained, in a phrase in which Yahweh himself is the subject, probably indicates that *rūaḥ yhwh* is here being used as a technical term; see Zimmerli, *Ezechiel* (BKAT), p. 886.

81. Eichrodt, *Theology of the Old Testament* I, pp. 410ff.

82. May has attributed the passages concerning the new spirit (11.14–21; 36.22–32; etc.) to 'the editor', as Hölscher and others have done.

83. F. Häussermann, *Wortempfang und Symbol in der alttestamentlichen Prophetie* (BZAW 58), 1932, pp. 4ff.

84. Alternatively vocalized *mar'eh* (masc.) and *mar'āh* (fem.).

85. A. R. Johnson, *The Cultic Prophet in Ancient Israel*, Cardiff ²1962, pp. 10f. and notes.

86. Zimmerli, *Ezechiel* (BKAT), p. 47.

87. Lindblom, *Prophecy in Ancient Israel*, pp. 83ff.

88. H. Schmidt omits the phrase 'in visions of God' as 'a fundamentally accurate gloss' in 8.3. Similarly in 11.24, 'in the vision, by the spirit of God' is omitted, although the following *hammar'eh* ('the vision') is retained. So also Fohrer and Eichrodt. (Schmidt, 'Hesekiel', *SAT* 2/2, in loc.; Fohrer, *Ezechiel* [HAT], in loc.; Eichrodt, *Ezekiel*, [OTL], in loc.).

89. So Eichrodt, op. cit., p. 112 n.111.

90. Bertholet believed Ezekiel 8ff. was based on observations made by the prophet when he was, in fact, in Palestine. Subsequent redaction has made it appear that Ezekiel was in Jerusalem *nur im Geiste* (*Hesekiel* [HAT], 1936, p. 29). From the observations 'in the spirit' recorded in chs 8 and 11, chs 9 and 10 should, however, be distinguished as truly visionary experiences.

The phrase 'in the spirit' cannot be allowed in any discussion of Ezekiel's experiences if, underlying it, there is conceived some form of 'body-spirit' dualism. Whether one rejects the translocations as literary figures or not, such allusions can only be understood as describing genuine sensations of removal or levitation (see below), or as instances of perceiving distant events by means of extraordinary, visionary capacities. When Elisha told of Gehazi's dealings with Naaman, he said it was his 'heart' (*lēb*) or 'spirit' (with RSV), which went forth (II Kings 5.26). By this Elisha implied that he himself perceived the event. We cannot define the prophet's understanding of the experience more closely, but here, as in the case of Ezekiel, we must reckon seriously with the concept of psychophysical unity characteristic of Old Testament thought; see Montgomery, *Kings* (ICC), p. 377; D. S. Russell, *The Method and Message of Jewish Apocalyptic* (OTL), 1964, p. 166; et al.

91. Widengren, *Literary and Psychological Aspects*, p. 103 (his emphasis).

92. R. H. Charles, *Apocrypha and Pseudepigrapha of the Old Testament* II, Oxford 1913, p. 210. Cf. also II Baruch 6.3 and the shorter recension of The Testament of Abraham, chs 7f., quoted by Russell, *Jewish Apocalyptic*, p. 167.

93. Similar ambiguity of expression is found in the Koran. Some Muslims contend Muhammad's night journey (*Sūra* 17) was made in the flesh, others that it was a visionary experience. See e.g. A. Kamal, *The Sacred Journey*, London 1964, pp. 106f. Jewish scholars differ in the same way as to the appropriate manner of understanding the tradition of Ḥagigah 14b concerning

the translocation of four Rabbis to heaven. See the Soncino *Babylonian Talmud, Seder Mo'ed* 8, London 1938, in loc.

94. Reading *d^emūt 'iš* in v. 2 with LXX.

95. Cf. the Apocryphal Bel and the Dragon, v. 36.

96. Op. cit., p. 106.

97. See the sympathetic discussion of this view in G. A. Danell's *Studies in the Name Israel in the Old Testament*, Uppsala 1946, pp. 239ff.

98. Jer. 7.8–15; 11.13; II Kings 23.31ff.

99. Each scene of the vision is introduced by a reference to the prophet being brought to a certain place. Each observation is preceded by *w^ehinnē* ('and behold'). The speeches of the guide each have an introduction, 'And he said to me', followed by the question, 'Do you see?' and the form of address, 'Son of man'. Measured progression of thought and location are evident as the prophet moves from outside the temple to the inner court, to see increasingly greater abominations.

100. On visionary experience in general, see Lindblom, *Prophecy in Ancient Israel*, pp. 36ff. Lindblom distinguishes 'hallucinations' from 'visions' and 'auditions' because, while a hallucination does not correspond to any objective reality in the external world, it 'is thought to be apprehended by the bodily senses and has all the characteristic features of a real perception' (op. cit., p. 123).

101. See F. Horst, 'Die Visionsschilderungen der alttestamentlichen Propheten', *EvTh* 20, 1960, pp. 193ff.

102. E.g. Isa. 6.1; cf. Jer. 1.11.

103. E.g. Amos 7.1; Jer. 24.1.

104. Num. 22.31; I Kings 22.17, 19; II Kings 6.17; 8.13.

105. Cf. Ezek. 1.27; 8.4; 40.4; etc. Horst (op. cit.) notes that even where forms of simple visual perception are used in Ezekiel they are apt to be elaborate, as, for example, in 1.4: 'As I looked, behold . . .'.

106. Interest in the prophet's life history is wholly subordinate to the interests of prophetic proclamation; see *Ezechiel* (BKAT), pp. 41, 104.

107. E. C. Broome, 'Ezekiel's Abnormal Personality', *JBL* 65 (1946), pp. 277ff.

108. Howie, *The Date and Composition of Ezekiel*, pp. 69ff.

109. Ezek. 12.6, 11; 24.24, 27.

110. See e.g. C. Richet, *Thirty Years of Psychical Research: being a treatise on metapsychics*, ET London 1923, pp. 546ff., D. J. West, *Psychical Research Today*, Harmondsworth 1962, pp. 75f.

111. See M. Buttenwieser, p. 8 of 'The Date and Character of Ezekiel's Prophecies', *HUCA* 7, 1930, pp. 1ff.; H. W. Hines, p. 53 of 'The Prophet as Mystic', *AJSL* 40, 1923–4, pp. 37ff.; Cl. Huart, *Les saints des derviches tourneurs* (Bibliothèque de l'École des Hautes Études, Sciences religieuses 32), Paris 1918, pp. 65, 289; Richet, op. cit.

112. See the Indices to the *Proceedings of the Society for Psychical Research*, London, s.v. 'Telekinesis; Levitation'. Also, the article, 'Report on a case of Table Levitation and Associated Phenomena', by K. J. Batcheldor, *Journal of the Society for Psychical Research*, vol. 43, no. 729, London, September 1966,

pp. 339ff.; and Celia Green, *Out-of-the-Body Experiences*, for the Oxford Institute of Psychophysical Research, London, 1968.

113. One outstanding account from a Rarongo student of the Western District of Papua tells how a famous sorcerer was asked if he would help a young girl living on a New Guinea island some 700 miles away by direct route. The sorcerer thereupon 'flew' to the girl, discussed her problem and returned. His return – within an hour – was signalled by his 'landing' on the roof of the parents' house. He reported on the girl's condition and she subsequently confirmed the appearance of the sorcerer in her room at the hour and on the day in question. Eliade claims that the experience of magical flight is common to all pre-literate societies (*Myths, Dreams and Mysteries*, p. 105). See also *Hallucinogens and Shamanism*, ed. M. J. Harner, Oxford 1973, p. 196: 'Flying: hallucinations of'.

114. W. Grey Walter, *The Neurophysiological Aspects of Hallucinations and Illusory Experience*, London 1960, p. 17. The possibility of employing narcotic drinks, flagellation, self-hypnotism, asceticism, etc., to similar ends is also noted by Buttenwieser, op. cit., and I. M. Lewis, *Ecstatic Religion*, Harmondsworth 1971, p. 39.

115. For a survey of Penfield's research see W. Penfield and L. Roberts, *Speech and Brain Mechanisms*, New Jersey and London 1959, esp. pp. 38–55 and 272f.

116. E.g. 'I had a dream, I wasn't here'; 'I have a queer sensation as if I am not here – as if I were half and half here' – Penfield, p. 342 of 'Some Observations on the Cerebral Cortex of Man', in the *Proceedings of the Royal Society of London*, Series B, vol. 134, London 1947, pp. 329ff.

117. There is no need at this point to deal further with these investigations. The relationship of the minor mental disturbances, referred to in the text, to more extreme disorders, including aphasia, is considered by Penfield however. The experiences underlying Ezekiel's symbolic immobility and dumbness (3.25f.; 4.4–8; 24.26f.), which a number of scholars consider to imply catalepsy, may be explicable in such terms. For references see A. Lods, *The Prophets and the Rise of Judaism*, ET London 1937, p. 215 n. 8.

118. Hughlings Jackson, a pioneer of modern neurophysiology, used the term 'dreamy state' of the condition in which the hallucinations, referred to above, occurred; see *Selected Writings of John Hughlings Jackson*, ed. James Taylor, London 1931–2. Psychical researchers refer to 'out of the body' experiences, in which individuals have the sensation of leaving their bodies and undertaking various activities independently of it. But though the gross physical manifestations of psychical phenomena, including corporeal levitation, which were popular in the nineteenth century are now reported to be 'very much out of fashion', a further comment in this regard is especially pertinent to study of Ezekiel: 'At this point of time, it requires an imaginative effort of some difficulty to project one's mind into a period when physical phenomena dominated the Spiritualistic scene', *Proceedings of the Society for Psychical Research*, vol. 54, no. 195, London, March 1964, p. 29.

119. See R. A. Nicholson, *The Mystics of Islam*, London 1914, esp. pp. 120ff. Cf. also n. 90 above.

120. The genitive (κυρίου) of II Cor. 12.1 is probably subjective, as *ᵉlōhim* is in Ezek. 8.3; 40.2; so Plummer, II *Corinthians* (ICC), 1915; F. V. Filson, 'II Corinthians', *IB* 10, in loc.

121. Widengren, *Literary and Psychological Aspects*, p. 103.

122. Ibid., p. 110.

123. Ezek. 11.1–21 has been added later to its present position.

124. Widengren, op. cit., p. 107.

125. Cf. May, 'Ezekiel', *IB* 6, p. 283. The basis of a genuine visionary experience involving the new temple can be discerned in 43.5, where *rūaḥ* lifts the prophet up and takes him to the inner court, to see the glory of Yahweh entering the temple.

126. As is assumed by Cooke, Howie, Muilenburg ('Ezekiel', *Peake's Commentary*, 2nd edn ed. Black and Rowley), Zimmerli, et al.

127. Dürr, *Die Stellung des Ezechiel in Apokalyptik*, pp. 25ff., though see too n. 90 above.

128. Buttenwieser, 'The Date and Character of Ezekiel's Prophecies', *HUCA* 7, 1930, p. 7.

129. W. Zimmerli, 'Das Wort des göttlichen Selbsterweises' (1957), *Gottes Offenbarung*, pp. 120ff.

130. Von Rad, *Der heilige Krieg*, pp. 7ff.; cf. Noth, *Josua* (HAT), ²1953, p. 137.

131. E.g., Judg. 20.28 (a priest); 3.28 (a judge); see again von Rad, op. cit., pp. 7f.

132. On the role of priests and prophets in military campaigns in the ancient Near East, see C. H. Gordon, *Ugaritic Literature* (Scripta Pontificii Instituti Biblici 98), Rome 1949, p. 125.

133. Cf. I Kings 21.29, where both a question is asked and a causal statement is offered as a basis for a prophetic judgment.

134. The German terms are those used by Zimmerli himself.

135. See further pp. 90ff., of Zimmerli's 'Erkenntnis Gottes nach dem Buche Ezechiel' (1954), *Gottes Offenbarung*, pp. 41ff.

136. 25.3–5, 6–7, 8–11, 15–17; 26.2–6; 29.6b–9a; 35.5–9; and others, with some peculiarities, see 'Das Wort', *Gottes Offenbarung*, p. 129.

137. Fohrer, 'Remarks on Modern Interpretation', *JBL* 80, 1961, p. 310; cf. his *Introduction*, p. 409. This too is his assessment of the origin of the references to 'the hand of Yahweh' in I Kings 18.46 and II Kings 3.15; see *Elia* (AThANT 53), ²1968, p. 55.

138. See e.g. Eissfeldt, *Introduction*, pp. 285ff., and p. 9 above.

139. Fohrer, *Introduction*, p. 232; cf. Eissfeldt, *Introduction*, p. 142.

140. J. Wellhausen, *Die Composition des Hexateuchs*, Berlin ³1899, pp. 283f.

141. See particularly Šanda, *Die Bücher der Könige* I (EH), p. 508; Gray, *Kings* (OTL). p. 424; although the latter's reluctance to admit the original coherence of vv. 35ff. with the Ahab narrative should also be noted (op. cit., p. 431).

142. See Burney, *The Hebrew Text of Kings*, pp. 207ff.

143. Von Rad, *Der heilige Krieg*, p. 54.

144. A variety of early passages refer to the delivery of Yahweh's enemies 'into the hand' of Israel's charismatic leaders, (e.g., Num. 21.34; Josh. 10.8; I

Kings 22.6). The motif of a few Israelites overcoming many opponents is found in such passages as Judg. 7.2ff. and I Sam. 14.6, while references to opponents of Yahweh as *hāmōn* ('a multitude') appear in Judg. 4.7; I Sam. 14.16; etc. Zimmerli examines the use of the phrase 'and you shall know that I am Yahweh' in Israel's early traditions and notes that the Yahwist used it, but only as an utterance of Yahweh himself, or of his messengers (see Ex. 7.17; 8.22; 10.2; cf. Num. 16.28–30), 'Erkenntnis Gottes', *Gottes Offenbarung*, pp. 61ff. Cf: also the expressions in I Kings 18.36f.; II Kings 5.15 et al., which are more freely formulated, suggesting their later origin.

145. See ch. I.B above.

146. '. . . Ezek. den auf das gottesdienstliche Geschehnis der Selbstoffenbarung Jahwes ausgerichteten "Kultpropheten" zuzurechnen ist,' Zimmerli, 'Das Wort des göttlichen Selbsterweises', *Gottes Offenbarung*, p. 128.

147. See Zimmerli, 'Ich bin Jahwe' (1953), *Gottes Offenbarung*, pp. 11ff.; Stamm, in J. J. Stamm and M. E. Andrew, *The Ten Commandments in Recent Research* (SBT 2.2), 1967, pp. 77f.

148. 'Elohim' appears for 'Yahweh' in the Elohistic Ps. 50.7.

149. In a similar inversion of the tradition of holy war, Jeremiah prophesied that Yahweh himself would fight against Jerusalem (Jer. 21.5f.).

150. The command is found nine times: with reference to the mountains of Israel, Ezek. 6.2; the false prophetesses, 13.17; the south, 20.46; Jerusalem, 21.2; Ammon, 25.2; Sidon, 28.21; Pharaoh, 29.2; Mount Seir, 35.2; Gog, 38.2.

151. Ezek. 4.3 and 7.

152. Num. 22.41; 23.13; 24.2.

153. Eissfeldt, *Introduction*, p. 54.

154. Fohrer, *Ezechiel* (HAT), p. 37.

155. See G. P. Kurath, *Funk and Wagnall Standard Dictionary of Folklore, Mythology and Legend* II, ed. M. Leach (New York, 1949–50), s.v. 'Overlooking', pp. 837f.; cf. also J. G. Frazer, *The Golden Bough*, London ³1935, s.v. 'Eye, the evil'; 'Evil Eye'; P. D. Chantepie de la Saussaye, *Lehrbuch der Religionsgeschichte*, ed. A. Bertholet and E. Lehmann, Tübingen ⁴1925, s.v. 'Blick, böser'; 'Auge, böses'.

156. Lindblom, *Prophecy in Ancient Israel*, pp. 48f.

157. Understanding '(and he set) his face toward Hazael'.

158. Keret I vi 37; cf. also Baal III iv 7; in G. R. Driver, *Canaanite Myths and Legends* (Old Testament Studies 3), Edinburgh 1956.

159. E.g. Baal II iv 20; Baal V iva 37 (ibid.).

160. See also I Kings 8.28f.; Pss. 13.1; 22.24; 27.9; et al.; Hos. 5.15; Isa. 54.8; 57.17; 59.2; 64.7; and cf. also Ezek. 39.23, 24, 29, which belong to the closing summary of Ezekiel's teaching. On the concept of Yahweh's 'face' (*pānîm*) in Israelite tradition, see W. Beyerlin, *Origins and History of the Oldest Sinaitic Traditions*, ET Oxford 1965, pp. 100ff., 155.

161. Cf. Lev. 26.17; Jer. 21.10; 44.11.

162. '. . . The sons of the prophets were sitting before [Elisha]' (II Kings 4.38); 'certain of the elders of Israel came and sat before me' (Ezek. 14.1); 'certain of the elders of Israel came to inquire of Yahweh and sat before me' (Ezek. 20.1); etc.

163. S. Herrmann, 'Die Königsnovelle in Ägypten und in Israel', *WZ Leipzig* 3 (1953–4), pp.51ff.

164. Zimmerli, *Ezechiel* (BKAT), p.209; 'The Special Character of Ezekiel's Prophecy', *VT* 15 (1965), p.518.

165. After the German *Königsnovelle*. See the discussion of the form in Egypt and the Old Testament in R. N. Whybray, *The Succession Narrative* (SBT 2.9), 1968, pp.98ff.

166. A. Jolles, *Einfache Formen*, Halle 1930, pp.62ff.; E. Otto, *Handbuch der Orientalistik* I. 2, ed. B. Spuler, Leiden 1952, pp.143ff.; Alfred Herrmann, *Leipziger Ägyptologische Studien* 10, ed. W. Wolf, Glückstadt-Hamburg etc. 1938, p.39, n.64.

167. Jolles, op. cit., pp.67f., 87f.

168. A. Bentzen, *Introduction to the Old Testament*, Copenhagen ²1952, p. 243.

169. G. von Rad, 'The Beginnings of Historical Writing in Ancient Israel' (1944), in *The Problem of the Hexateuch*, pp.166ff.

170. There is also significant variety in the scenes described at the opening of the Egyptian 'royal novels' referred to by S. Herrmann.

171. See Gunneweg, *Mündliche und schriftliche Tradition*, pp.77f.

172. Montgomery, *Kings* (ICC), p.369.

173. II Kings 6.32; Ezek.8.1; 14.1; 20.1; cf. 33.31.

174. See the appendix *Justice in the Gate* (1931), in L. Köhler, *Hebrew Man*, ET London 1956, pp.149ff.

175. Judg.20.26; 21.2; II Sam.7.18 (cf. I Chron.17.16); Ps.61.7; and perhaps Ps.140.13.

176. M. Newman, pp.94ff. of 'The Prophetic Call of Samuel', in *Israel's Prophetic Heritage*, ed. B. W. Anderson and W. Harrelson, New York and London 1962, pp.86ff.

177. Ex.19.3–8; Josh.24.14–15; I Sam.12.14–15.

178. J. Muilenburg, 'The "Office" of the Prophet in Ancient Israel', in *The Bible in Modern Scholarship*, ed. J. P. Hyatt, London 1966, pp.74ff.; Newman, op. cit.; et al.

179. Carley, *Ezekiel's Place in Prophetic Tradition* (Diss., London University 1968), pp.31ff., and see p.53 below.

180. See von Rad, *Old Testament Theology* II, pp.395ff.; W. Zimmerli, *The Law and the Prophets*, ET Oxford 1965, pp.67ff.

III. EZEKIEL AND OTHER MAJOR STREAMS OF OLD
TESTAMENT TRADITION

1. See particularly M. Burrows, *The Literary Relations of Ezekiel*, Philadelphia 1925; Fohrer, *Die Hauptprobleme*.

2. See ch.I. D.

3. Hos.2.8, 13; 8.4; cf. Ezek.16.11f.

4. Hos.2.10; Ezek.16.37; cf. Ezek. 23.29; Lam.1.8, where Jerusalem's nakedness is said to be revealed by the ravages of her enemies.

5. H. Gese, p. 146 of 'Bemerkungen zur Sinaitradition', *ZAW* 79, 1967, pp. 137ff.

6. So R. Bach, *Die Erwählung Israels in der Wüste* (Diss., Bonn 1952), reviewed in *ThLZ* 78, 1953, col. 687.

7. Talmon, pp. 46f. of 'The "Desert Motif" in the Bible', in *Biblical Motifs*, pp. 31ff.

8. Cf. Ezek. 23.19.

9. Cf. Hos. 2.15b; Jer. 2.2f.

10. Against J. W. Flight, 'The Nomadic Idea and Ideal in the OT', *JBL* 42, 1923, pp. 158ff.

11. See Talmon, op. cit., particularly p. 50; also Wolff, *Hosea* (BKAT), pp. 40, 55.

12. On the archaic character of covenant formulae with the preposition *le*, see J. Begrich, p. 5 of 'Berit. Ein Beitrag zur Erfassung einer alttestamentlichen Denkform', *ZAW* 60, 1944, pp. 1ff.

13. Though cf. v. 28, where it is implied that the wild beasts will not actually be removed, but will no longer devour the people.

14. Wolff, p. 319 n. 3 of 'Jahwe als Bundesvermittler', *VT* 6, 1956, pp. 316ff.

15. The verb *ʿālāh* 'go up' in v. 11 may then be related to its usage in Ezra 1.3, 5; 7.7; Neh. 7.6, – so e.g. Robinson and Horst, *Die zwölf kleinen Propheten* (HAT), [2]1954, p. 7.

16. Wolff, 'Der grosse Jesreeltag (Hosea 2.1–3)' (1952), *Gesammelte Studien*, pp. 160ff.

17. Retaining the MT's *melek*, since it corresponds with *mamelākhōt* in the same verse.

18. So G. Beer, *Exodus* (HAT), 1939, p. 14 etc.

19. Zimmerli, *Ezechiel* (BKAT), p. 908.

20. Herntrich, *Ezechielprobleme*, p. 130.

21. Burrows, *Literary Relations*, p. 15.

22. J. W. Miller, *Das Verhältnis Jeremias und Hesekiels sprachlich und theologisch untersucht*, Assen und Neukirchen 1955.

23. P. R. Ackroyd, *Exile and Restoration* (OTL), 1968, p. 51.

24. Cf. Eichrodt, *Ezekiel* (OTL), p. 13; et al.

25. T. H. Robinson, 'Baruch's Roll', *ZAW* 42, 1924, pp. 209ff.; Eissfeldt, *Einleitung in das Alte Testament*, Tübingen 1934, pp. 17f.; ET of 3rd ed., 1965, pp. 16f. and 350ff. Cf. also W. O. E. Oesterley and T. H. Robinson, *An Introduction to the Books of the Old Testament*, London 1934, pp. 304ff.; and now J. Bright, 'The Prophetic Reminiscence: its Place and Function in the Book of Jeremiah', *OuTWP*, 1966, pp. 11ff.

26. Miller, op. cit., pp. 21ff. A very different explanation of the Jeremiah prose tradition is advanced by E. W. Nicholson, *Preaching to the Exiles*, Oxford 1970, on which see p. 79 below.

27. Jer. 2.4–13; 3.6–11; cf. Deut. 1–11. The scroll may have begun with the account of the prophet's commissioning and the reason for his action in having the record of his prophecies declared in public (Jer. 36.1–3; 1.4–19).

28. Jer. 7.2–8.3; cf. Deut. 12ff.

29. Jer. 11.2–5; cf. Deut. 27.15ff. The formula *ʾārūr hāʾiš* ('cursed be the man') is used in common.

30. Jer. 13.1–11, 12–14; 14.11–16; 15.1–4a; 16.1–9; 18.1–12; 19.1, 2a, 10, 11a; cf. Deut. 28.15ff.

31. Jer. 25.1–13; cf. Deut. 29.2–30.20. A summary of affairs, immediately following the reading of the law, is also found in Jer. 11.9–14; cf. Deut. 26.16ff.

32. Cf. Jer. 3.6ff.; 7.21ff.; etc.; see also Lindblom, *Prophecy in Ancient Israel*, pp. 357ff.

33. See particularly the conditionals in vv. 5–7 (cf. 26.4–6) – and J. Muilenburg, 'The Form and Structure of the Covenantal Formulations', *VT* 9, 1959, p. 365.

34. See ch. II.F above.

35. See e.g. H. H. Rowley, 'The Prophet Jeremiah and the Book of Deuteronomy', in *Studies in Old Testament Prophecy presented to T. H. Robinson*, ed. H. H. Rowley, Edinburgh 1950, pp. 157ff.=*From Moses to Qumran*, London 1963, pp. 187ff.; M. Sekine, 'Davidsbund und Sinaibund bei Jeremia', *VT* 9, 1959, pp. 47ff.

36. Cf. H.- J. Kraus, *Worship in Israel*, ET Oxford 1966, pp. 199f.

37. Cf. Jer. 16.4 and Deut. 28.26.

38. Miller, op. cit., pp. 52f.

39. See H. Wildberger, *Jahwewort und prophetische Rede bei Jeremia* (Diss., Zürich 1942), esp. pp. 29f., 32f.; von Rabenau, 'Die Entstehung des Ezechiel', *WZ Halle* 5 (1955–6), pp. 664ff.

40. Wildberger reduces the seven minor variants of this formula to two. One of these we have quoted in the text, and the other is the same, but cast by the narrator into indirect speech (op. cit., pp. 19ff.).

41. So Jer. 13.2, 5, 7; 28.15; 32.9ff.; Ezek. 3.23; 12.7; 24.18f.; see G. Fohrer, *Die symbolischen Handlungen der Propheten* (AThANT 25), 1953, pp. 56f.

42. S. Mowinckel, 'Zur Komposition des Buches Jeremia', *Videnskapsselskapets Skrifter*, II Hist.-Filos. Klasse, 1913, no. 5, Kristiania 1914, p. 58.

43. Cf. Miller, op. cit., p. 81.

44. So Jer. 1.2, against Hyatt, 'Jeremiah', *IB* 5, pp. 779ff., who regards this as the date of the prophet's birth.

45. See Skinner, *Prophecy and Religion*, p. 237, n. 1; Bright, *Jeremiah* (AB), 1965, pp. 181f.

46. Miller attempts to establish an early date for these chapters (op. cit., pp. 65f.), following Volz and Rudolph, and cf. Eissfeldt (*Introduction*, pp. 361f.). But Bright observes stylistic similarities between some verses and Deutero-Isaiah (op. cit., pp. 284ff.).

47. While a number of scholars have called in question 'some of the most dreary and repetitious prose sections' of Ezekiel (R. H. Pfeiffer, *Introduction to the Old Testament*, New York 1941, p. 564; cf. Bertholet, *Hesekiel* [HAT], 1936, p. XIV; May, 'Ezekiel', *IB* 6, pp. 50f., 62), the absence of repetitiveness is by no means a satisfactory criterion of authenticity. Elliger has observed, with respect to the *Grundschrift* of the Priestly narrative, that repetition betrays the importance of the subject for the author (pp. 129f. of 'Sinn und Ursprung der priesterlichen Geschichtserzählung', *ZThK* 49, 1952, pp. 121ff.).

48. For a number of examples see Miller (op. cit., pp. 81ff.), and the references there to the more detailed lists in the studies of K. Gross, *Die*

literarische Verwantschaft Jeremias mit Hosea, Berlin 1930, p. 28; and S. R. Driver, *Introduction*, pp. 297f.

49. See H. Schmidt, 'Die grossen Propheten', *SAT* 2/2, p. 391; Zimmerli, *Ezechiel* (BKAT), pp. 16ff.

50. The hithpa'el form of the root *nb'* is only used in canonical prophecy by Jeremiah and Ezekiel.

51. The word *'āḥōt* is found in prophecy only in Jeremiah, Ezekiel and Hos. 2.1.

52. Oesterley and Robinson, *Introduction*, p. 305. Such is also said to be the relationship of Ezek. 18 to Jer. 31.29–30.

53. Cf. T. H. Robinson, 'Baruch's Roll', *ZAW* 42, 1924, pp. 217f.

54. Von Rad, *Old Testament Theology* II, p. 235.

55. '. . . are being committed': the masc. pl. participle *'ōśim* occurs in Old Testament prophecy only in Jer. 7.17; 26.19; 32.30; 44.7; Ezek. 8.6, 9, 12, 13; 33.31.

56. Zimmerli regards Jer. 15.16 and Ezek. 3.1–3 as the passages which most clearly reveal a literary relationship (*Ezechiel* [BKAT], p. 69*).

57. See in particular Fohrer, *Die Hauptprobleme*, pp. 135ff.

58. Robinson, op. cit.

59. J. Skinner, *The Book of Ezekiel* (Expositor's Bible), London 1895, p. 15.

60. Bright, 'The Prophetic Reminiscence', *OuTWP*, 1966, pp. 29f.

61. Fohrer, *Introduction*, p. 42.

62. So H. Haag, *Was lehrt die literarische Untersuchung des Ezechiel-Textes?*, Freiburg/Schweiz 1943, pp. 124, 137ff.

63. See Burrows, *Literary Relations*, pp. 19ff.; Fohrer, *Die Hauptprobleme*, pp. 140ff.; and cf. Cooke, *Ezekiel* (ICC), pp. xxxif.; E. Balla, *Die Botschaft der Propheten*, ed. G. Fohrer, Tübingen 1958, p. 284.

64. Cf. Noth, p. 8 n. 11 of 'The Laws in the Pentateuch' (1940), in *The Laws in the Pentateuch and other Essays*, pp. 1ff.; S. R. Driver, *Introduction*, pp. 73ff., 145; et al.

65. A. C. Welch, *Deuteronomy, the Framework of the Code*, Oxford 1932, pp. 2, 196ff.

66. So e.g. L. Elliott-Binns, 'Some Problems of the Holiness Code', *ZAW* 67, 1955, pp. 26ff.; M. Noth, *Leviticus*, ET (OTL), 1965, p. 15; although Eissfeldt concedes that at least part of the material may have come from sanctuaries outside Jerusalem (*Introduction*, p. 238).

67. Ezek. 6.3f.; 16.16; cf. 6.13; 20.27ff. The latter passages appear to have been enlarged upon in terms of the references in Deuteronomy and Jeremiah to profanities committed 'under every leafy tree' (Deut. 12.2; Jer. 2.20; 3.6; etc.; cf. Hos. 4.13). Ezek. 6.3f., 13 also recall the threat of Lev. 26.30f.; see H. Reventlow, *Wächter uber Israel: Ezechiel und seine Tradition* (BZAW 82), 1962.

68. Against Haag, op. cit., pp. 130ff.

69. H. Reventlow denies that H demands centralization on the grounds that the law regarding slaughter before 'the tent of meeting' reflects the actual conditions of the wilderness period, *Das Heiligkeitsgesetz formgeschichtlich untersucht* (WMANT 6), 1961, pp. 18f. Elliott-Binns, on the other hand, argues that the references to both 'the tent of meeting' and 'the tabernacle of

Yahweh' are Priestly interpolations in Lev. 17.1–9 (op. cit., pp. 30ff.). Certainly the view that all slaughter was sacrificial argues against centralization.
70. Ezek. 16.40; 23.47.
71. So Burrows, *Literary Relations*, p. 19; Fohrer, *Die Hauptprobleme*, p. 144; although the latter considers Ezek. 23.47 to be a later addition to the text.
72. Deut. 10.9; 18.2; cf. Num. 18.20.
73. Burrows, op. cit., p. 20.
74. Deut. 10.8; 17.12; 18.5, 7.
75. Haag, op. cit., pp. 48f.
76. See further H. McKeating, 'On Understanding Ezekiel', *The London Quarterly and Holborn Review*, London 1965, pp. 36ff.
77. Fohrer, *Ezechiel* (HAT), pp. 61f.; S. Herrmann, *Die prophetischen Heilserwartungen im Alten Testament* (BWANT 5/5), 1965, pp. 244ff.
78. *Wächter über Israel*, pp. 5 off.
79. On the rendering 'new heart' for the MT's 'one heart' in Ezek. 11.19, see Herrmann, *op. cit.*, p. 245, n. 3; Reventlow, op. cit., p. 53, n. 59.
80. See p. 56 above.
81. See E. Nielsen, *Shechem. A Traditio-historical Investigation*, Copenhagen ²1959, p. 267; de Vaux, *Ancient Israel*, pp. 362f.
82. H. Gese, *Der Verfassungsentwurf des Ezechiel (Kap. 40–48) traditionsgeschichtlich untersucht*, (BHTh 25), 1957, p. 49. For details of the present paragraph see also pp. 21f., 57ff.; and cf. Gunneweg, *Leviten und Priester*, pp. 188ff.
83. On the distinction between the terms *bayĩt* and *miqdāš* in Ezek. 40–48, see Gese, op. cit., pp. 26f.
84. Cf. Cornill, *Das Buch des Ezechiel*, p. 228.
85. Burrows, *Literary Relations*, pp. 30ff.; Fohrer, *Die Hauptprobleme*, pp. 144ff.; S. R. Driver, *Introduction*, pp. 49ff., 130ff., 145ff.
86. E.g. Driver, op. cit., p. 149; O. Procksch, *Theologie des Alten Testaments*, Gütersloh 1950, p. 306; Burrows, op cit., p. 36.
87. E.g. C. H. Graf, *Die geschichtlichen Bücher des Alten Testaments*, Leipzig 1866, p. 81; L. Horst, *Leviticus 17–26 und Hezekiel*, Colmar 1881, p. 96.
88. Cf. B. Baentsch, *Das Heiligkeits-Gesetz, Lev. 17–26*, Erfurt 1893, pp. 81ff.
89. Fohrer, *Die Hauptprobleme*, p. 147; *Introduction*, p. 142.
90. Von Rad, *Studies in Deuteronomy*, pp. 25ff.; Reventlow, *Das Heiligkeitsgesetz*.
91. Von Rad, op. cit., p. 31.
92. Cf. *KBL*, s.v. *kī* II.
93. Accounting for *bᵉtōkēk* as a gloss; cf. Reventlow, *Wächter über Israel*, pp. 11 n. 36; 12 n. 38.
94. See Reventlow, *Das Heiligkeitsgesetz*, pp. 142ff.
95. Cf. C. Kuhl ('Die "Wiederaufnahme" – ein literarkritisches Prinzip?', *ZAW* 64 [1952], pp. 1ff.), who regards this manner of resuming prophetic addresses simply as evidence of later redactional interpolation.
96. Cf. Ezek. 34.25 and Lev. 26.5f.; Ezek. 34.26f. and Lev. 26.4, etc.
97. As, for example, H. G. May does, 'Ezekiel', *IB* 6, p. 56.

98. Fohrer, *Die Hauptprobleme*, p.148 and n.67.
99. S. R. Driver, *Introduction*, p.146.
100. H. Reventlow, *Das Amt des Propheten bei Amos* (FRLANT 80), 1962; *Liturgie und prophetisches Ich bei Jeremia*, Gütersloh 1963.
101. This view is criticized on pp.4f. above and p.74 below.
102. Reventlow, *Wächter über Israel*, p.159, cf. p.43.
103. Especially Ezek.16; 20; 23.
104. Reventlow, op. cit., p.116.
105. Ibid., pp.127ff., 167.
106. On the themes of the primary tradition developed in Ezek.16.44–58 and 16.59–63, see Zimmerli, *Ezechiel* (BKAT), p.342, and cf. Reventlow, op. cit., p.91.
107. Zimmerli, 'Erkenntnis Gottes', *Gottes Offenbarung*, p.108.
108. Fohrer, *Die Hauptprobleme*, pp.135ff., and see now Zimmerli, *Ezechiel* (BKAT), pp.66*ff.
109. Wolff, *Hosea* (BKAT), p.176.

IV. CONCLUSION

1. Jer.29.8f., 15, 21–23, 31f.
2. Bright, 'The Prophetic Reminiscence', *OuTWP*, 1966, pp.11ff.
3. The form of the verb with which 37.1–14 begins suggests that a statement of the date once preceded that vision too; see Zimmerli, *Ezechiel* (BKAT), pp.891f.
4. Ibid., p.41.
5. The problems raised by such a criterion are outlined by T. W. Overholt, *The Threat of Falsehood: A Study in the Theology of the Book of Jeremiah* (SBT 2.16), 1970, p.39 n.28.
6. See ch.II.C above.
7. See Carley, *Ezekiel* (Cambridge Bible), 1974, p.326: 'Ezekiel, book of: exposition etc.'
8. Ch.II.D.
9. See p.25 above.
10. M. Noth, *A History of Pentateuchal Traditions*, ET Englewood Cliffs, N.J., 1972, p.167.
11. Ex.18.13ff.; 24.1a, 9–11; Num.11.16ff. respectively.
12. Cf. J. Fichtner, col.77 of 'Jesaja unter den Weisen', *ThLZ* 74, 1949, cols 75ff.
13. See Ch.II n.117 and ch.IV n.34.
14. Lindblom, *Prophecy in Ancient Israel*, p.123. For the relationship of hysteria to ecstasy, see Lewis, *Ecstatic Religion*, pp.192f., 200–203.
15. H. B. Huffmon, p.123 of 'Prophecy in the Mari Letters', *BA* 31, 1968, pp.101ff.
16. R. A. Knox, *Enthusiasm*, Oxford 1950.
17. Ch.II.F.
18. Lewis affirms the strong link between ecstasy and conditions of social instability, *Ecstatic Religion*, pp.203f.; from the sociological viewpoint,

ecstasy may appear as attention-seeking behaviour designed to gain leadership, ibid., pp. 32, 151, 192f.

19. J. T. Nichol, *The Pentecostals*, Plainfield, N.J., 1971, p. 66.

20. Knox, op. cit., pp. 2, 581.

21. E.g. I Kings 20; see also Zimmerli, 'Das Wort des göttlichen Selbsterweises', *Gottes Offenbarung*, p. 126.

22. See H.-E. von Waldow, *Anlass und Hintergrund der Verkündigung des Deuterojesaja*, Bonn 1953, pp. 119ff.

23. See pp. 32, 40 above.

24. The words 'the priest', in apposition in Ezek. 1.3, may refer to either Ezekiel or his father. It is possible that 'the thirtieth year' in 1.1 indicates Ezekiel's age and was intended to establish his authority as a priest, since according to Num. 4 members of priestly families could undertake priestly duties from the age of thirty.

25. Cf. Lev. 17.3, 8, etc.

26. Reventlow, *Wächter über Israel*, pp. 157f.

27. J. Wellhausen, *Prolegomena to the History of Israel*, ET Edinburgh 1885, p. 398.

28. Ibid.

29. P. R. Ackroyd, *Continuity: a contribution to the study of the Old Testament religious traditions*, Oxford 1962, p. 19.

30. R. Rendtorff, 'Botenformel und Botenspruch', *ZAW* 74, 1962, pp. 165ff.; J. F. Ross, 'The Prophet as Yahweh's Messenger', in *Israel's Prophetic Heritage*, ed. Anderson and Harrelson, pp. 98ff.

31. R. E. Clements, *Prophecy and Covenant* (SBT 1.43), 1965, p. 81.

32. Reventlow, op. cit., p. 157. It is also relevant here to note Gevirtz's criticism of applying modern criteria of creativity and originality to ancient poetry: 'Rather is it in the reworking of old themes by means of conventional phraseology, in traditional manner, to reproduce familiar actions uniquely and poetically significant that the poet's genius is to be sought', *Patterns in the Early Poetry of Israel* (Studies in Ancient Oriental Civilization 32), Chicago 1963, p. 14.

33. Ch. III.D.

34. On the complicated traditions of Ezekiel's dumbness and immobility, see Carley, *Ezekiel* (Cambridge Bible), pp. 28–32.

35. On entrance liturgies, see ch. I n. 29 above; on individual responsibility in Ezekiel, see B. Lindars, 'Ezekiel and Individual Responsibility', *VT* 15 (1965), pp. 452ff.

36. See p. 64 above.

37. See p. 39 above.

38. Mowinckel, *The Psalms in Israel's Worship*, ET Oxford 1962, II p. 57.

39. Cf. Amos 7.14 which suggests there was a recognized distinction between 'professional' and 'lay' prophets, as there was in Mari.

40. Gunneweg, *Mündliche und schriftliche Tradition*, pp. 81ff. and particularly pp. 115ff.

41. See pp. 7f., 24f., 26–28 and 67–69 above.

42. Mowinckel, 'The "Spirit" and the "Word"', *JBL* 53, 1934, pp. 199ff.; for similar emphasis on ethical criteria as means of distinguishing the classical

reform prophets from the 'national-demagogic' prophets, who unduly emphasized Yahweh's promises to bless and protect his people, see E. Osswald, *Falsche Prophetie im Alten Testament* (Sammlung gemeinverständlicher Vorträge und Schriften aus dem Gebiet der Theologie und Religionsgeschichte 237), Tübingen 1962, esp. p. 22.

43. Overholt, *The Threat of Falsehood*, pp. 42–44.
44. Cf. von Rad, *Old Testament Theology* II, p. 236.
45. See pp. 11 and 46f. above.
46. See p. 28 above.
47. See pp. 26f. above.
48. Ch. I.D.
49. Ackroyd, *Exile and Restoration*, p. 71.
50. On which see ch. III.B above.
51. E. W. Nicholson, *Preaching to the Exiles.*
52. See pp. 48 and 62 above.
53. See pp. 12 and 46 above.
54. Healing: 47.12; peace: 34.25.

INDEX OF AUTHORS

INDEX OF BIBLICAL REFERENCES